THE PUTNEY DEBATES

This essential new series features classic texts by key figures that took center stage during a period of insurrection. Each book is introduced by a major contemporary radical writer who shows how these incendiary words still have the power to inspire, to provoke and maybe to ignite new revolutions . . .

THE PUTNEY DEBATES

THE LEVELLERS

INTRODUCTION BY GEOFFREY ROBERTSON QC

TEXTS SELECTED AND ANNOTATED BY PHILIP BAKER

VERSO
London • New York

First published by Verso 2007
Introduction © Geoffrey Robertson 2007
© in the selection and editorial matter Verso 2007
All rights reserved

The moral rights of the author have been asserted

3 5 7 9 10 8 6 4

Verso
UK: 6 Meard Street, London W1F 0EG
USA: 180 Varick Street, New York, NY 10014-4606
www.versobooks.com

Verso is the imprint of New Left Books

ISBN-13: 978-1-84467-175-5

British Library Cataloguing in Publication Data
A catalogue record for this book is available from the British Library

Library of Congress Cataloging-in-Publication Data
A catalog record for this book is available from the Library of Congress

Typeset in Bembo by Hewer Text UK Ltd, Edinburgh
Printed and bound in the UK by CPI Group (UK) Ltd, Croydon, CR0 4YY

CONTENTS

INTRODUCTION

THE LEVELLERS: THE PUTNEY DEBATES

Geoffrey Robertson QC

'Our cause and principles do through their own natural truth and lustre get ground in men's understandings so that though we fail, our truths prosper. And posterity we doubt not shall reap the benefit of our endeavours.'

John Lilburne, 'England's New Chains Discovered', March 1649

Gordon Brown, in his first week as Prime Minister, offered to vouchsafe his country a written constitution.[1] All too few of his countrymen knew that the first draft was debated 360 years ago, at a crucible moment when a nation emerging from a brutal civil war against an autocratic monarch was free to contemplate a new form of government. That debate, over the Levellers' 'Agreement of the People', took place in a church in Putney, on the edge of the River Thames, part way between the parliament at Westminster and Runnymede, the island of Magna Carta. It was chaired by Oliver Cromwell and its outcome, against his more conservative instincts, was a resounding victory for what in those days was pejoratively described as 'democracy', a revolutionary idea that most parliamentarians of the time believed would lead to anarchy. From its first ascendancy in that Putney church there may be traced the acceptance – centuries later in the Universal Declaration of Human Rights and now in two thirds of the nations of the world – of the idea that government requires the consent of freely and fairly elected representatives of all adult citizens, irrespective of class or caste or status or wealth. Today's single most important political principle, the right to live in a participatory democracy, comes down to us not from the slave-owning societies of Athens and Rome, or from the pleasant estates in France where Rousseau and Montaigue envisioned the 'general will', but from buff-coated and blood-stained English soldiers and tradesmen. This book lets their voices resonate again, in the hope that their passion may inspire those in Britain who now want to 'make it appear to the world at how high a rate we value our freedom'.[2]

It is an abiding irony that the United Kingdom, a country that has more history to be proud of than any other, should be so reluctant to acknowledge the most significant part of it. The civil war years, 1641–9, first established what today are regarded as universal values – the supremacy of parliament, the independence of the judiciary, the abolition of torture and of executive courts, comparative freedom of speech and toleration of different forms of religious worship. Yet we allow our children to leave school at sixteen knowing nothing of this period: they study (if they study optional history at all) the rise and fall of Hitler and the rise and rise of the United States: the struggle of civil rights takes place, in their curriculum, in Little Rock and Mississippi, never at Naseby or Putney. They are permitted to notice the civil war in passing, at the age of thirteen, when the government education website[3] (designed, apparently, by unreconstructed royalists) enjoins teachers to focus on Cromwell as a man of vengeance, through 'violent incidents' in that 'year of reckoning' of 1649. It was a year described by parliament at the time as 'the first year of freedom, by God's blessing restored,' and it is a serious indictment of those charged to teach our children well that they fail to teach them at all about the principles of representative government that were established in this era, or about those who fought and died for them.

History that is taught through the indulged lives of kings and queens cannot cope with the reality of a British republic: it is euphemistically called 'The Interregnum' and the men who led it are demonized as 'regicides'. In fact, they had no alternative but to remove Charles I if the fundamentals of representative government were to be observed in England, because he was incorrigible in planning war on his own people to restore his supreme power. It was during the debates at Putney that he began to be described as 'a man of blood', whose punishment was not so much a matter of 'cruel necessity' as a matter of justice. Anachronistic distaste for the king's execution must not obscure the remarkable political developments inspired by the Levellers that preceded it. Charles I had the purest form of sovereign immunity – he was the sovereign – yet the message that went out from the debates at Putney, that the law was no respecter of persons, eventually put him in the dock.

'An Agreement of the People', the set of constitutional proposals debated in late October and early November 1647, was the work of 'Levellers', a group not easy to define, either as a political collective or as architects of a coherent constitutional programme. Their individual leaders frequently changed allegiances and political positions. The movement emerged in London towards the end of the civil war, initially in support of the charismatic John Lilburne – Freeborn John – a favourite of the crowd for his magnificent defiance of the Star Chamber. They were essentially polemicists and pamphleteers rather than politicians, notable for scattergun criticism of all who wielded power, whether the king himself or leaders in the parliament and the army or in the city guilds. Their constituency in this new era of press freedom was drawn from literate tradesmen and soldiers engaged by arguments over what form government should take and readily influenced by satirical jeremiads against the unrepresentative nature of the House of Commons, with its rotten boroughs and its unequal electorates, under a franchise that allowed votes only to men of landed property. As Puritans who craved liberty of conscience, the Leveller writers despised the Presbyterian MPs who looked to restoration of the monarch as the means of imposing their religion upon the kingdom. As proponents of 'free trade' (i.e. abolition of guilds and monopolies), their cause rallied independent merchants and tradesmen. By urging fair treatment and immunity for soldiers who had successfully fought against royal tyranny, they found a ready constituency among the ranks of an army threatened with disbandment.

The New Model army, victorious for parliament in the first civil war, had set up a General Council, on which its leaders (Fairfax, Cromwell and Cromwell's son-in-law Henry Ireton) sat with soldiers' representatives (called 'agents' or, in a neutral sense, 'agitators'). In the autumn of 1647 Leveller-inspired dissent had reached such a pitch that the leaders invited these representatives, together with some of the civilian Levellers who were fanning it, to a council meeting at St Mary's church in Putney to thrash out their differences. The Generals ('grandees' as Lilburne mockingly called them) intended to debate 'The Heads of the Proposals', the settlement terms that they had put to the king, requiring him to share some power with a parliament elected on the same narrow franchise as before. Instead, on the eve of the debate, the Levellers printed and circulated 'An Agreement of the People', a simple and moving charter calling for a more representative parliament, for freedom of conscience and religious toleration, and for an end to all discrimination on grounds of 'tenure, estate, charter, degree, birth or place'. In a calculated rebuke to the Generals for their meetings with the monarch who had started the civil war, the 'Agreement' bemoaned the 'woeful experience' of being 'made to depend for settlement of our peace and freedom upon him who intended our bondage and brought cruel war upon us'.

By tabling the 'Agreement', the Levellers and their allies hijacked the debate. After an initial spat over whether it would be right for the army to alter the position taken in 'The Heads of Proposals', the argument moved on the second day to the subject of the franchise. The immortal exchanges were between lawyer Henry Ireton, Cromwell's cautious son-in-law, who feared that universal male suffrage would lead to the destruction of private property, and Colonel Thomas Rainborough, a radical army officer who may never have read a Leveller pamphlet but who famously extemporised the case for democracy: 'I think that the poorest he that is in England hath a life to live, as the greatest he; the poorest man in England is not at all bound in a strict sense to that government that he hath not had a voice to put himself under' The upshot of this debate was a show of hands in favour of extending the vote to all free men, i.e. to all Englishmen except beggars, servants and women (the poorest she would not be enfranchised). The meeting then moved on to the king, a subject that became so heated and potentially treasonable that Cromwell stopped the shorthand writer so there would be no record of the first demands for prosecution of 'the man of blood', currently under their watch at Hampton Court. Cromwell, the great temporiser, had not yet given up hope of reaching an accommodation with Charles, but the patience of his army colleagues was beginning to run out. Why, they asked, if God had meant us to negotiate with the king, was he proving so stubborn?

For all Oliver Cromwell's subsequent conflicts with the Levellers and their ideas, his openness in engaging in the Putney debates and his liberality in chairing them – he denied no one the floor and suffered with dignity some wounding criticism – is much to his credit. Henry Ireton, the Leveller's chief protagonist, may have been on the wrong side of history by insisting that the franchise be limited to men with a 'fixed proprietary interest' in the nation, but his power of argument leaves little doubt that his early death in Ireland in 1651 robbed the republic of Cromwell's natural successor. The Leveller-inspired insubordination in the army was quickly quashed, but their proto-democratic ideas survived and Lilburne went on to make mighty contributions to freedom of expression and the right to defy abuses of government power. The Putney debates were not published at the time, but a transcript was prepared by the shorthand writer, and discovered in the archives of his Oxford College centuries later. It provides a fascinating snapshot of the hearts and minds of men who had fought the civil war for freedom of speech and of conscience, as they struggle to define the form of government that would best safeguard their victory.

The texts selected for this book were written and spoken in the years 1646–9 by men who had sharp experience of Stuart absolutism: Lilburne himself had been whipped and tortured by order of the king's Star Chamber. Now that the royalists had been beaten, radical writers were suffering intimidation and imprisonment by parliament for their attacks on the Presbyterian MPs who dominated the House of Commons. Understandably, the Levellers had a prejudice against power and all who exercised it: the rhetoric in 'A Remonstrance of Many Thousand Citizens' (Text 1) and 'The Large Petition' (Text 2) is addressed to parliament, to remind it of the abuses suffered under Charles I, who must not be put back on the throne without the firmest safeguards against repetition. These two pamphlets, which the censors tried to suppress, remind their readers (who were more numerous in consequence) of the evils of the Stuart monarchy and the stupidity of the Presbyterian MPs who were seeking to restore it. Republican in logic if not in terms, these early post-war publications remind us of the paradox of the time: the king was the enemy commander under house (in fact, mansion) arrest, but he remained the king. Parliament had seen him 'with obstinate violence, persisting in the most bloody war that this nation ever knew', yet here it was 'begging and entreating him in such submissive language to return to his kingly office as if it was impossible for any nation to be happy without a king'. At Putney, it was Rainborough who would ask the question: 'I would fain know what the soldier hath fought for all this while?' In these texts, the Leveller writers Overton and Walwyn argue that they fought to be rid of all the abuses of power identified with Charles I – abuses the like of which they were now beginning to suffer at the hands of the parliamentary Presbyterians. They leave open the crucial question, on which the Levellers were later to divide, namely whether they should rid themselves permanently of monarchical government.

The Leveller polemicists draw upon a shared sense of the constitutional struggles that came after Elizabeth I had been succeeded in 1603 by James Stuart, king of Scotland and a true believer in his God-given right to rule as an absolute prince, through his executive court of Star Chamber and through bishops who controlled the church. His claim to overrule judges was contested by his Chief Justice, Edward Coke, who pointed out that God's prodigy he may be, but 'the law is the golden metewand and measure to try the causes of your Majesty's subjects, and it is by that law that your Majesty is protected in safety and in peace'. The king aimed a punch at this unruly jurist, who ducked and grovelled and was later sacked for insubordination.[4] Charles succeeded to the throne in 1625, imbued with his father's absolutist beliefs but lacking his skill at avoiding conflict with parliament, whose puritan squires – men like Elliot, Pym and Hampden – asserted against him Coke's vision of the common law as no respecter of persons and of Magna Carta as the guardian of liberty. They were imprisoned for their defiance, but returned to parliament in 1629 to pass 'The Petition of Right' – a bill of rights drafted by Coke – and to condemn the king for illegal taxation and denial of *habeas corpus*. Charles had their leaders arrested and thrown into the Tower, and refused for the next eleven years to summon another parliament.[5]

The ensuing years of the king's personal rule (1629–40) were marked by further attempts to impose unlawful forms of taxation like ship money, and by a ferocious determination to enforce religious orthodoxy. Congregationalists whose individual consciences could not abide bishops or their stained-glass attitudes left for Massachusetts (some 30,000 crossed the Atlantic in the 1630s) or formed sullen and powerful opposition networks. The Star Chamber sought to deter open opposition by use of torture: notoriously, in 1637 it cut off the ears and branded the foreheads of three puritan leaders and sent them to prison for life. A vast crowd gathered around their pillory and one hot-headed youth was inspired by their speeches to distribute their seditious works. John Lilburne was arrested and hauled before the Star Chamber: famously, he refused to answer any questions, claiming that as a freeborn Englishman he was entitled to his right against self-incrimination. The Star Chamber ordered him to be whipped all the way from Fleet Street to Westminster – a sentence carried out viciously before a large crowd who cheered this courageous young man, whom they dubbed 'Freeborn John'.[6]

Eventually, the king was forced to summon parliament as a means of financing a war to impose religious orthodoxy on the Scots. Pym, Hampden and the puritan lords who had previously opposed him were not prepared to vote new taxes – they had returned more determined than ever to share his power. After the king's ignominious defeat by the Scots, they impeached his advisors and proceeded to abolish ship money, the Star Chamber and other royal prerogatives (such as the power to dismiss judges at will and to issue warrants for torture) and to pass a *Grand Remonstrance* – an indictment of his government for breaching the liberties of his subjects laid down in Magna Carta and the Petition of Right. Charles advanced on the Commons to arrest Pym and four other leading MPs, only to find 'the birds have flown' – to a city of such militant Protestantism that Charles soon abandoned it for a new capital, Oxford. Pym had led the defiant parliamentarians, but it had not been long before a 'sharp and untunable voice' was heard from an unknown MP, demanding the release of John Lilburne. It is one of the minor ironies of the time that Oliver Cromwell's maiden speech was to demand the release from prison of the man who would become his tormentor-in-chief.

The king declared war on parliament in August 1642 – his 'cavaliers' (a pejorative reference to 'caballeros', Spanish troopers given to torturing Protestants) matched against 'roundheads' (from the crop-eared city apprentices who supported parliament, or possibly from John Pym's round and balding head). Towns, counties and families were split in their allegiance, although cavalier officers tended to be men of birth and status, while the middle rank of the parliamentary army came to reflect Cromwell's famous preference ('I had rather have a plain russet-coated captain that knows what he fights for, and loves what he knows, than that which you call a gentleman and is nothing else.') The royalists had the best of the first year's fighting, thanks to the dashing Prince Rupert of the Rhine, until Pym, dying of cancer and in desperation, brought in the Scots army with a promise that parliament would, if victorious, make Presbyterianism the official religion – a Kirk of England. The turning point came with the battle of Winceby, in October 1643, when Rupert's hitherto unbeaten cavalry was routed by the parliamentary horse, commanded by two officers who had never before fought together: Oliver Cromwell and Sir Thomas Fairfax had begun their sensational partnership, which continued the following year at Marston Moor with 5,000 royalist deaths ('God made them as stubble to our swords'). It was then that a significant political divide opened in the parliamentary leadership between those who wanted to make peace with the king on minimal terms, and those like Cromwell who believed that a constitutional settlement would only hold if the king was resoundingly defeated first. This loosely corresponded to a Protestant division in parliament itself, between 'peace party' Presbyterians and 'war party' Independents who were Congregationalist in their preference of worship and keener to limit monarchical power. (At this point, only one MP was a republican, and he was sent to the Tower for admitting as much: no one else could conceive of government other than by 'King, Lords and Commons'.)

In 1645, the New Model army was created as a professional fighting force led by Fairfax with, at his insistence, Cromwell as his deputy. It had a war aim that brooked no appeasement: to advance Christ's kingdom and to 'bring to justice the enemies of our church and state'. In just one year, these well-trained, hymn-singing 'ironsides' were formidable enough to win the battle of Naseby and, in effect, the war: by early 1646 Fairfax had Oxford surrounded and the king made his ignominious exit, in disguise, to surrender to the Scots, who sold him to a parliament whose Presbyterian majority were prepared to welcome him back on condition that he imposed their religion on the nation. But there was now another rival institution capable of exercising power in the land, and which was much more democratic – the New Model army. It was led by generals who were Independents, leading men who had for years suffered appalling privations, who had seen their comrades killed or maimed in battle and who looked to parliament for recompense – a body now dominated by a party which feared them, refused to pay or indemnify them, and wanted them disbanded (or sent to Ireland) as soon as possible. It was, for soldiers who had risked their life in the parliamentary cause, a strange kind of victory.

★

John Lilburne, on his release from prison, had joined the parliamentary army and fought bravely at Edge Hill, but when captured and taken to Oxford as a prisoner of war, found himself put on trial – for treason. This was a breach of the laws of war, which protect prisoners from punishment other than for war crimes. When parliament heard of this royalist outrage it passed a Declaration: it would put captured cavaliers on trial for treason if Lilburne's execution went ahead. But could this news reach Oxford in time to save him? There was no telephone, fax or carrier pigeon at Westminster, and no open line of communication between the forces. So Lilburne's heavily pregnant wife, Elizabeth, persuaded the Speaker to give her an authenticated copy of the Declaration and set off via horseback for Oxford, reaching the city in the nick of time – the king relented and Freeborn John was freed. He took a commission in Cromwell's troop and fought bravely at Marston Moor, but with the king beaten he returned to London to face a more formidable foe – the parliamentary Presbyterians. As the policy gap between these dour and repressive conservatives and the much more liberal Independents began to widen, John Lilburne began to pour ink on troubled waters.

The Presbyterian policy was to deliver upon Pym's promise to the Scots to unite the two kingdoms in Kirk-based worship. They executed the Anglican Archbishop, William Laud, then moved against the Congregationalists. Censorship of the press was re-imposed, inspiring the Independents' most eloquent spokesman, the poet Milton, to utter his immortal cry for press freedom, the *Areopagitica* (licensing the press was akin to 'the exploit of that gallant farmer who sought to keep out the crows by shutting his park gate'). Like sleaze-ridden British politicians today, these MPs reached for the libel laws to gag their critics. Lilburne was the most vitriolic, although he was soon joined by other skilled writers and phrasemakers like Richard Overton (author of 'A Remonstrance') and William Walwyn (who drafted 'The Large Petition'). These original 'Levellers' (the name, which they resented, began as a royalist smear during the Putney debates[7]) were in truth freelance journalists, who threw themselves into political propaganda for the radical wing of the parliamentary Independents. Their cause, asserted first against the king and then against the Presbyterians, was liberty of conscience and liberty of trade: lacking in birth or wealth or any political authority, they revelled in the power of their own words as it moved thousands of tradesmen and apprentices, who purchased their tracts for a penny at London bookshops and taverns.

They had plenty of sticks to beat the government, initially by recalling the abuses of power by the king, whom parliament now wanted to restore without safeguards against repetition. Then they moved on, as investigative journalists, to expose the corrupt Presbyterian leaders who controlled the city council in the interests of its wealthy members. Lilburne's first demand for annual elections by all free men was made in

'The Charter of London': the poorest as well as the richest, he said, should have a say in electing the Lord Mayor. He was already a charismatic orator, and Overton was the pseudonymous author of the *samizdat* 'Martin Marpriest' pamphlets, whilst Walwyn was a more withdrawn figure who supplied money and printing presses as well as sober and persuasive prose. Lilburne was soon imprisoned for libel, and Overton followed him to the Tower, but they had no difficulty in smuggling out a series of seditious and provocative tracts, immediately printed on clandestine presses, with titles like 'England's Misery and Remedy'; 'England's Birthright Justified'; 'Protestation and Defence of Lieutenant John Lilburne'; 'The Just Man in Bonds'; 'The Arrow against All Tyrants'; 'Royal Tyranny Discovered'. The more efforts made by parliament to suppress them the more popular they became, in a city whose people were increasingly asking, as taxes and prices rose: 'What have we fought for all this time?'

That same question was being asked, and much more bitterly, in the army, which had sustained in the civil war a comparatively higher loss of life than was suffered in the trenches of the First World War. Soldiers had expected some respect from the institution for which they had fought, but instead parliament was determined to smash the New Model before it became a power-base for independency. The Presbyterian plan was to provide but niggardly recompense to its soldiers, to cut back pay and refuse them indemnity for war damage and then to disband most regiments and send the rest to fight the king's supporters in Ireland. By 1647, soldiers and officers alike were disenchanted with this treatment and the Leveller pamphlets were avidly read by the campfires and distributed by a network of supporters organized by Edward Sexby. 'Lilburne's freedom – soldiers' rights' became a slogan for a distinct political movement that sprang to life in various regiments in the spring of 1647. Soldiers in each regiment elected representatives (the 'agitators') to take their grievances to the officers. The army *en masse* at a 'rendez-vous' at Newmarket made a solemn 'Engagement' that they would not suffer themselves to be disbanded until their grievances were met. They issued a stirring declaration:

that we were not a mere mercenary army, hired to serve any arbitrary power of state, but called forth and conjured by the several declara-tions of parliament to the defence of our own and the people's just rights and liberties.

They also set up a Council upon which two officers and two soldiers selected from each regiment would serve along with the High Command, to debate army policy and ensure consultation with the rank-and-file (after the army encamped in London, it became in effect 'the Putney debating society').[8] Its first business in July 1647 was to settle 'The Heads of the Proposals' (Text 3) that Cromwell and Ireton would put to the king, who had conveniently been taken into the army's custody a few weeks before and was now ensconced with his retinue at Hampton Court. It was a surprisingly moderate document that required the king to summon a new parliament every two years. It would deprive him of control of the armed forces for ten years, but his royalist officers were to have an amnesty, and would be debarred from public life only for five years. The *Proposals* demanded religious liberty: bishops were to be deprived of authority and never again could the king impose the Book of Common Prayer or any other Anglican orthodoxy, whilst the Presbyterian covenant could never be enforced against an individual's conscience. Otherwise, the king and queen and their royal issue would be 'restored to a position of safety, honour and freedom in this nation without further diminution or limitation to the exercise of regal power'.

This was an astonishingly generous offer by the civil war victors but Charles, besotted by his own belief that he had been divinely appointed as an absolute monarch and deviously preparing his supporters for a second civil war, deliberately duchessed the army leaders, playing them off against their parliamentary rivals. This was not difficult: the Presbyterian MPs had recently dismissed an army petition with such contempt (their 'Declaration of Dislike') that their ingratitude had entered into the souls of both soldiers and officers, who responded with charges of corruption against the main Presbyterian leaders. Ill feeling in Westminster reached such a state in August, after a Presbyterian mob attacked Independent MPs, that Fairfax apprehensively led his forces into London. It turned, however, into a victory parade: there was a fine show of trumpeting and drumming, greeted with 'huzzahs' from an excited public thronging their route. Fairfax made his way to the Tower and called for its copy of Magna Carta: 'This is that which we have fought for and by God's help we must maintain.'[9] A few weeks later Cromwell himself visited the prison, ostensibly to inspect its ordinance but really to visit Lilburne and offer a deal: his release in return for his support for the army, or at least his silence. Freeborn John, by now feeding the grievances of a network of disaffected soldiers with pamphlets condemning 'grandees' like Cromwell for treating with the king, refused his offer. The army set up its headquarters at Putney and on the surface an autumnal calm descended on the city: Lilburne's own lawyer, John Cooke, captured the optimism of the moment in the title of his latest book, *A Union of Hearts between the King's Most Excellent Majesty, the Right Honourable Lords and Commons in Parliament, His Excellency Sir Thomas and the Army under his Command; the Assembly and Every Honest Man that Desires a Sound and Durable Peace, Accompanied with Speedy Justice and Piety.*

★

The moment passed, in a London on whose chessboard the three contending powers – king, parliament and army – were in watchful play. At Westminster, the Presbyterians were still in the majority and bent on negotiating a settlement with the king that would establish their religion, although (thanks partly to Lilburne's efforts) they were weakened when the Independents took the city council at the September elections. The army was encamped at Putney, its leaders trying to negotiate a different settlement with the king to provide for liberty of conscience. The king, at Hampton Court, patiently played off both sides while secretly planning a new war, in which the Scots would invade to restore him to the throne in return for eradicating Baptists and Quakers and other emerging religious sects that were tolerated by the Independents. It was to the credit of the Levellers that they saw through the king's duplicity, the parliament's stupidity and the generals' naivety, all of which they exposed in a series of scorching pamphlets hot from presses hidden in the quarters of sympathetic soldiers, who subscribed 4 pence (half their daily wage) to pay for the print and for its delivery to regiments in other parts of the country.

The inspiration came from Lilburne's prison cell; the logic from Walwyn who was at large, whilst the most inflammatory work was contributed by John Wildman, a 24-year-old republican lawyer with a savage turn of phrase and nerves of steel that he was soon to show by crossing verbal swords with Ireton. Edward Sexby, another powerful Leveller voice at Putney, was an agitator who contributed to the writing and organized the distribution of pamphlets. But even the most subversive example of all this agitation – the Wildman/Sexby 'Call to All the Soldiers of the Army' (Text 5), called only for the king's 'speedy impeachment': it had nothing to say about a trial, let alone an execution. Their real target was Ireton, who had been duchessed by Charles and who had led the General Council of the army to reject their demands. In a suddenly chilling passage, the *Call* incites disaffection:

> with a word you can create new officers. Necessity has no law, and against it there is no plea. The safety of the people is above all law. And if you be not very speedy, effectual, and do your work thoroughly, and not by halves as it has been, you and we perish inevitably.

For all this mutinous muttering, the pamphlet that precipitated the Putney debates was 'The Case of the Army Truly Stated' (Text 4), the Levellers' response to Ireton's 'Heads of the Proposals'. They objected to dealing with the king, both on the ground that he could not be trusted and because the 'Proposals' would allow him too much power. They condemned both the parliament and the army leaders for offering settlements that maintained the king's 'negative voice' – his right to veto new legislation. But what was truly revolutionary about 'The Case of the Army' was their demand that 'all the freeborn at the age of 21 years and upward be the electors' except for 'delinquents' (i.e. royalists). This was the first demand to extend the parliamentary franchise beyond the traditional 40-shilling freehold-land requirement, and to place the vote in the hands of all freeborn adult males. It had been inspired by Freeborn John, but put together by the less flamboyant hands of some of the agitators who signed it, and it was none the worse for plain speaking. It may indeed have been this very quality – its lack of customary Leveller abuse and exaggeration – that persuaded Fairfax that its authors' 'intentions were honest' and that it made enough sense to warrant discussion in the army's General Council, which met every Thursday in the church at Putney. Such was the speed and professionalism of the Leveller printers that by the time of the council's next meeting on 21 October, 'The Case of the Army' was on the bookstalls and Cromwell had already dissociated the army leadership from it in a speech in the Commons. The Council referred the document to a committee, which invited the army agitators who had signed it to send representatives to explain it at the next meeting of the General Council, on Thursday, 28 October.[10]

Over the intervening week, the agitators and their civilian supporters produced a document unlike any that had gone before: a short statement which set out the rights of every Englishman freely and fairly to choose representatives to a parliament with supreme power to pass laws and

THE PUTNEY DEBATES

make war, and which could be constrained only by a set of five fundamental and unalterable rights that it could not deny to any citizen:

1. Liberty of conscience in matters of religion ('The ways of God's worship are not at all entrusted by us to any human power.')
2. Freedom from conscription (since 'money, the sinews of war' is always at parliamentary disposal, it should never force citizens to fight).
3. A general amnesty to all who had fought on either side of the civil war.
4. That all laws must be 'no respecter of persons but apply equally to everyone: there must be no discrimination on grounds of tenure, estate, charter, degree, birth or place'.
5. Parliament could pass no law 'evidently destructive of the safety or wellbeing of the people'.

In short, 'An Agreement of the People' (Text 6) was offered as a draft constitution for a government as democratic as the times could conceive, comprising a sovereign parliament bound only by the inalienable right of all citizens to equality and to religious liberty.

By what stroke of genius had the army malcontents and their civilian propagandist allies suddenly hit upon a written constitution, guaranteeing a sovereign parliament and a set of basic civilian rights that parliament could not alter, as the way forward? John Lilburne was in this week preoccupied with his own appearance before a House of Commons committee and his literary flourishes are absent from the measured language of 'the Agreement', although he is likely to have suggested 'extracting some principles of common freedom' that would be unalterable by parliament ('These things we declare to be our native rights (as) the freeborn people of England'). Most historians detect the more measured draftsmanship of William Walwyn, assisted by the legal insight (but not the political petulance) of young Wildman. Their tactical triumph was to replace the lengthy and less inspired 'Case of the Army', already denounced by Cromwell, with a short and more inspiring agenda for the debate. 'The Agreement', delivered to the council by the Agitator Robert Everard on the day before the meeting, was solemnly read aloud at its outset. It may have been the reason why Fairfax, the Council's chairman, called in sick, since he was anxious to keep himself above controversy, as a commander venerated by all the troops (a loyalty he was later to exploit at Cork Bush Field and Burford). It would also explain why the usually decisive Ireton appears off balance on the first day, and Cromwell genuinely and impartially inquisitive – his lugubrious mind seems to be mulling over the fact that a written constitution might not be a bad idea at all.

It was, of course, an idea that much later took some shape in the Bill of Rights of 1689, and a more precise and potent form in the US Constitution. But for all that 'An Agreement of the People' might serve as a rough precedent for Jefferson's 'self-evident truths', it was presented at Putney by a group of soldiers who had yet to convince their commanders, let alone their parliament. The Presbyterian MPs, when they had their chance to debate *The Agreement* in the Commons a few weeks later, ignorantly condemned it as 'destructive to the being of parliament, and to the fundamental government of the kingdom'. Of course, there was nothing 'destructive' to government in the proposal to do away with rotten boroughs or to extend the franchise to all free men, while the natural law notion of inalienable rights protected by the judiciary had been developed by Coke: his *Institutes* (Lilburne's favourite law book) argued that no political power could override *habeas corpus*, the common law or Magna Carta. But what *The Agreement* omitted was the subject upon which nobody, including the Levellers, could agree – the future constitutional role (if any) of the sovereign.

'The Agreement' made no reference to the House of Lords: it defined 'parliament' as that body chosen by the people of England in electorates 'proportioned according to the number of inhabitants' with a sovereign power to enact and repeal laws. The other striking omission from *The Agreement*, by comparison with all other tracts of the time, was excessive reference and deference to God: He was mentioned only in the Preamble as 'having so far owned our cause as to deliver the enemies thereof into our hands' (a providentialist belief shared by Cromwell) and as moving in ways so mysterious to human comprehension as to preclude any government-imposed system of worship. Otherwise the inspiration is John Cooke's 'right reason' – the recognition that the 'principal right most essential to our wellbeing' is clarity and certainty in the extent of parliamentary power. It was the obscurity of that power which had led to the civil war, so a written constitution was essential to define it, in a way which would protect the people both from corrupt parliamentary majorities who might pass laws infringing fundamental rights and (this was unstated) from any sovereign who might claim to be above the law.

'The Agreement's' fourth guarantee, of equality for all, meant that the law was no respecter of persons – a principle which would soon be urged to justify the trial of the king.

And so the Army Council proceeded to its great debate on 28 October 1647, at the Putney church packed with 'agitators and officers, and civilians invited by the soldiers (Text 7). William Clark, a young clerk in the army secretariat who had developed a form of shorthand, was detailed to take the notes. Cromwell began by offering the floor to any comer, and Edward Sexby took it to make a forceful prepared statement, accusing the leadership of trying to be all things to all men except their own soldiers. They had laboured to please a king who would not be pleased unless they cut their own throats and a parliament whose majority consisted of rotten members. Told to his face that his 'credit and reputation has been much blasted', Cromwell was nonetheless emollient. He pointed out that the meeting had been called to discuss 'The Case of the Army Truly Stated', but since 'the Agreement' had now been tendered, they might as well consider it. Robert Everard, who had brought it to the council, came forward and read it aloud (Clark, not recognizing him, describes Everard by reference to his 'Buff Coat' – which he wore, no doubt, against the autumnal chill). This reading had an instant and favourable impact on the audience – 'The pretensions in it, and the expressions in it, are very plausible', Cromwell immediately concedes. It was 'specious' and 'plausible', but presaged 'very great alterations of the very government of the kingdom'. It required time to consider the consequences: 'there will be very great mountains in the way of this' he muttered – and the first of these was the fact that it seemed inconsistent with the army's previous 'engagement' at Newmarket in June to support the existing king and parliament.

Wildman immediately jumps to his feet, sensing that Cromwell's tactic is either to stall or, more dangerously, to dismiss 'the Agreement' (as he had already dismissed 'The Case of the Army') on the grounds that to support it would be inconsistent with the army's pre-existing New-market 'engagement'. There can be no obligation to stick by the letter of a previous undertaking, Wildman argued, if a more just and honest solution later becomes available. Henry Ireton – the leadership's big hitter – weighs in to crush the young civilian ('Sure this gentleman has not been acquainted with our engagements') but then Colonel Rainborough, whose language is imbued with moral conviction, argues that bad undertakings may be amended with good conscience: 'Have you death before you, the sea on each side of you and behind you – and are you convinced that the thing is just, I think you are bound in conscience to carry it on'. The procedural question was eventually resolved by setting up a committee to examine whether and to what extent *The Agreement* was consistent with the army's previous engagements, and the meeting decided (to Wildman's agnostic dismay) to begin the next morning with a prayer meeting at the house of the Quartermaster-General. That was where, the following afternoon, the momentous debate over the franchise was held.

It was started by Henry Ireton, whose prayers had made him combative, and determined to avoid the procedural shadow-boxing of the previous day. Having heard 'the Agreement' read again, the meeting proceeded to consider its uncontroversial first clause, requiring a fair distribution of electorates in proportion to the population – a demand that had been made by Ireton himself in paragraph 5 of 'The Heads of Proposals'. He knew that the Levellers had previously urged that all freeborn men should have the vote at age twenty-one (this was in paragraph 5 of *The Case of the Army*, but had not been spelled out in 'the Agreement') so he opened by throwing down the gage: did 'the Agreement envisage' this revolutionary principle, or were elections still to be conducted as they had for centuries, allowing votes only to those who had freehold worth more than 40 shillings? It was Colonel Rainborough who then rose so magnificently to this bait, with a short speech that stated the democratic principle with a passion engendered by five hours of prayer:

> . . . the poorest he that is in England has a life to live, as the greatest he; and therefore truly, Sir, I think it's clear, that every man that is to live under a government ought first by his own consent to put himself under that government; and I do think that the poorest man in England is not at all bound in a strict sense to that government that he has not had a voice to put himself under . . .

Ireton at first tried to dismiss this approach as based on a theory of 'birthright' that entitled an Englishman merely to breathe the air and travel the highways: the right to vote depended on whether he could in doing so acquire enough 'fixed local interest', i.e. land – to have a stake in government. Rainborough took notes of Ireton's somewhat legalistic arguments and rose magisterially to dismiss them: firstly, God gave reason to all men irrespective of whether they acquired land worth 40 shillings, for the very purpose that they should use that reason to decide which representatives to elect to parliament. Secondly, since the people are the foundation of all laws, all the people were entitled to a say in making them. Thirdly – and this went down well with the soldiers in the audience, many of whom had lost their estates in fighting for God and parliament – were they therefore to have no say in the new government? Ireton, in his turn, resorts to the 'floodgates' argument: unless the vote was confined to those with some permanent property, the result would be anarchy – men with no money might vote to redistribute the property of others to themselves. Rainborough takes great exception to being described as an anarchist, and points out that fidelity to God's law ('Thou shalt not steal') would prevent expropriation.

Cromwell hastily intervenes to cool tempers. 'Of course you are not an anarchist,' he assures Rainborough, but universal franchise might tend to anarchy 'if men that have no interest but the interest of breathing' are given the vote. Ireton, somewhat shaken by Rainborough's invocation of the Ten Commandments, is forced to say that 'divine law extends not to particular things' – a position that most puritans, who saw the hand of God in everything, would have been hard put to accept. But Rainborough plays to his audience: 'I would fain know what we have fought for: for our laws and liberties? [Yet] this is the old law that enslaves the people of England – that they should be bound by laws in which they have no voice at all!' When others in the audience manage to get a word in edgeways, their contributions support Rainborough rather than Ireton.

The requirement of a freehold worth 40 shillings disenfranchised small tradesmen and those with cash rather than land, or with leasehold rather than freehold, and even Cromwell soon comes to accept, in the flow of the debate, that those who inherit leaseholds should be enfranchised and that 'The Heads of the Proposals' was defective in not calling for electoral reform. Ireton, his back against the wall, sets up a straw man – the foreigner who might vote on a brief visit to England – but his opponents stick to the principle of the franchise as a birthright. Wildman points out that since government depends upon the free consent of the people, those denied the right to express that consent by voting cannot be said to be under a just government. Rainborough asks the familiar question: 'I would fain know what the soldier has fought for all this while – to give power to men of riches, men of estates, to make him a perpetual slave?' Ireton vainly tries to point out that what they had fought against was the king and his absolutist principle that 'one man's will must be law' but it was too late: Cromwell's chaplain, Hugh Peters, interjects that any soldier who helped to save England from Charles I was worthy of a voice in government. He suggests – and Cromwell gratefully accepts his suggestion – that a committee should resolve the extent of franchise reform. This was agreed, but not before concessions were made on both sides. Ireton admitted that his chief concern was that electors should not be persons who could be pressured by those on whom they depend, and Wildman's civilian colleague Maximilian Petty agrees with this position: servants and apprentices should therefore be excluded, as well as beggars who are dependent upon the charity of others.

A debate polarized at the outset had, many hours later, reached an almost consensus position: the vote should be granted to all adult males, excepting servants, foreigners, apprentices and beggars and (it so went without saying that it was not said) women. A straw vote was taken on this position before the meeting adjourned and only three voices were raised against it.[11] So this remarkable day of thesis and antithesis ends in a compromise driven by the logic of argument: the nation should become a democracy of independent men. Women were not considered be-cause, by the standards and laws of the time, they were assumed to be under their husband's direction – on this very basis Lilburne had recently secured his wife's acquittal for distributing his seditious works (he afterwards described her as 'the gravest, wisest and fittest messenger I could think of, and though a Feminine, yet of a gallant and true masculine spirit').[12] Although Ireton lost the argument, the force with which he put the case for maintaining the landed property qualification demonstrates how obvious it seemed to the ruling classes of the time. In this sense, the Putney debates were a landmark in thinking through democracy.

There was, however, a much more vexed problem that Cromwell could no longer ignore, and on which the Levellers were themselves divided. It was the question of the king: not just the warmongering Charles I, but the monarchy itself. Wildman and Sexby were republicans at heart, but Rainborough was not and on 31 October, during a lull in the debates, he visited John Lilburne in the Tower, to complain about the 'foolish zeal' of these disciples. Lilburne, who had become friendly with royalist prisoners, was sympathetic: his mission was to curb all power, whether in a kingdom or a republic. The next day's debate began with another lengthy prayer meeting, but the divine inspiration that came to some officers was that the reason for their distractions and divisions was quite simply God's displeasure: He had demonstrated this dislike of kings by sending them victorious, and was annoyed that they still wanted 'to preserve that man of blood' and the 'principles of tyranny' that any monarchy entailed. Wildman, ever the provocateur, suggested that God's dislike extended to the House of Lords as well – if power resided in the people through elections, as they had agreed on the previous day, then it could hardly extend to the aristocracy. Cromwell agreed that 'we all apprehend danger from the person of the king and from the Lords' but in these unsettled times they should cling to what was left of constitutional authority 'if it be but a hare swimming over the Thames, I will take hold of it rather than let it go'.

The debate continued in desultory and unminuted fashion for another week, when the Generals agreed to arrange an army 'rendezvous' to consult the troops. The last committee hearing took place on 11 November – the very day when the king took his destiny into his own hands by escaping from army custody at Hampton Court, so as to be at liberty to rally his Scottish supporters. He arrived at the Isle of Wight with a ready-made excuse for his flight: 'A people called Levellers', he told the islanders, were planning to overthrow him. Cromwell decided that the king must for the present be kept safe, under lock and key at Carisbrook Castle. At this juncture, the patience of the Generals gave out: the king was a loose cannon, with supporters-in-arms in Scotland and Ireland and on the continent, and it was no time to tolerate dissent. The promised army rendezvous was carefully laid as a trap for the insubordinates in the ranks. A limited number of regiments were invited to Cork Bush Field, where Fairfax eloquently rallied them as Cromwell rode about, tearing up copies of 'An Agreement of the People' that some wore in their hats. A potential mutiny was firmly put down and its leaders were court-martialled. The troops fell into line behind Fairfax, a beloved commander who promised to 'live and die with the army'. Leveller influence was checked, and the organization of agitators through which it had spread was broken, although the power of their ideas was to gather momentum and Lilburne was yet to have his finest hour.

*

The post-Putney story may briefly be told. The second civil war, planned by the king from his castle arrest at Carisbrook, eventually came in the summer of 1648, with invasion by the Scottish army co-ordinated with royalist uprisings in Essex. The army, now united against a common enemy, was again victorious – Cromwell famously so when his 'ironsides' vanquished a Scottish force three times its size at the battle of Preston, after which Fairfax crushed the royalist revolt in the south at the siege of Colchester. This time, Ireton and Cromwell could not allow 'the man of more blood' to plot a third civil war. The credulous Presbyterian MPs were still in a parliamentary majority and were, incredibly, still prepared to trust Charles: at Newport in November they actually negotiated his return to the throne. It was Henry Ireton who now reached out to the Levellers – his adversaries at Putney – to help him argue their most revolutionary proposal. They met at the Nag's Head Tavern in London, along with Hugh Peters and John Cooke, to draw up 'The Remonstrance of the Army', which stated that there could be no peace without justice on 'the capital and grand author of our troubles'. 'The Remonstrance' marked a new stage in the debate over the king – the emerging recognition that justice, rather than expediency, required the trial and punishment of Charles I, not only as retribution for the blood he was responsible for shedding, but as a deterrent to any future 'grand delinquent'.

Even at this point, the Levellers could not agree on the way forward: Lilburne insisted that the army should first accept 'An Agreement of the People' before moving against the king, whilst Wildman and Overton could not have it move quickly enough. The news that galvanized the army was of the tragic death of the popular and valiant Colonel Rainborough, slain by marauding royalists. The time had come to treat the king as the enemy commander: the interests of justice and the interests of peace in the nation conjoined to demand that Charles Stuart be brought to trial. In 'Prides Purge', the army and the independent group of MPs excluded the pig-headed Presbyterians from the House of Commons, thereby securing an independent majority for a parliament quickly dubbed, and always remembered, as 'the Rump'.

The Levellers, for all their democratic ideals and early rhetoric in favour of calling the king to account, fell strangely silent at this climactic moment. Freeborn John left London, like most of the lawyers and judges who were seized with terror at the prospect of involvement in the earth-shattering business of prosecuting the sovereign. The man who accepted the brief was Lilburne's lawyer, the barrister John Cooke, who charged the king with the crime of 'tyranny' – making war on his own people and presiding over plunder of their towns and torture of prisoners of war.[13] On 20 January 1649, just over a year after the Putney Debates, Charles I was brought before 'a High Court of Justice' comprising seventy leading citizens, in front of thousands of his subjects packed to the rafters of Westminster Hall. He was still very much a king in command: when the presiding judge motioned for the prosecutor to begin, the king prodded Cooke with his cane and gave the order 'Hold'. Cooke – the son of a Leicestershire share-cropper – ignored the royal command, but it was repeated with a more emphatic poke, followed by a third blow from the king's cane, hard enough to dislodge its silver tip which fell to the floor between the two men. The king ordered Cooke to pick it up, but the barrister refused and opened the case against Charles Stuart, 'In the name and on behalf of the people of England.' Slowly and painfully, under the astonished gaze of his people, the defendant stooped to pick up the silver tip. The symbolism was plain to all: his majesty had bowed before the majesty of the law. 'Be ye ever so high, the law is above you' had been an empty aphorism, but in this defining historical moment, Lilburne's lawyer had delivered on the promise of proposition 5 of 'An Agreement of the People': the law was no respecter of persons, and Charles I had at last been levelled.

Events proceeded rapidly thereafter. Cromwell and Ireton had no fixed plan to execute the king: providence, as it emerged in the course of the proceedings, would determine his fate. It did: Charles refused to recognize the court; he showed no remorse for the carnage of the civil war and every intention of provoking another. To save lives, the court decided that his had to be forfeited (a miscalculation, as it turned out, which made him a martyr and paved a sentimental way for his son's restoration eleven years later). The Levellers did not applaud the king's trial and execution – that was left to John Cooke (in 'The Case a Against the King') and to the more felicitous prose of John Milton, soon to become Cromwell's chief spin doctor, in *The Tenure of Kings and Magistrates*. Instead, they watched and waited, while the High Court of Justice declared (on 22 January 1649) that the House of Commons was the sole repository of legislative power and that its ordinances would henceforth become law without the consent of the king or the House of Lords. It The Commons soon abolished what it termed 'the office' of king ('To have the power thereof in any single person is unnecessary, burdensome and dangerous to the liberty, safety and public interest of the people') and eradicated the 'useless and dangerous' House of Lords. The Act making England a commonwealth declared the House of Commons 'the supreme authority of this nation, the representatives of the people in parliament' with executive government entrusted to a Council of State comprising the army commanders, a group of MPs, five peers and three judges. The coinage was reissued, imprinted with the declaration that 1649 was 'the year of freedom, by God's blessing restored'.

But the level of freedom, in this nation that had so suddenly become a republic, did not have the Leveller's' blessing. In 'England's New Chains Discovered' (Text 8) Lilburne was quick to voice his apprehensions that the members of the Council of State would fit into the jack-boots of the Star Chamber, that 'the Rump' would not submit itself to an election, and that censorship of the press was returning to protect 'the grand contrivers', Cromwell and Ireton, who were defaming their opponents as anarchists and 'levellers' (names 'both contradictory in themselves and altogether groundless in relation to the men so reputed'). Already the new regime was beginning to suppress uncomfortable thought: it had moved against the theologian John Fry in direct infringement of the liberty of conscience required by 'The Agreement'. They had provided for 'the stopping of our mouths' by permitting army generals to punish unlicensed printers, 'dealing with us as the bishops of old did with the honest puritan'. But for all the dangers from the corruption that inevitably attaches itself to political power, the Levellers had discovered one safeguard, a cause that they would henceforth famously champion as the most fundamental right of all: trial by jury. The 'high courts of justice' appointed to try the king and his senior commanders, and the potential legal powers of the Council of State, threatened to alter 'the usual way of trials by twelve sworn men of the neighbourhood', which was 'that great stronghold of our preservation' laid down by Magna Carta.

It was trial by jury that was soon to become Lilburne's own salvation, as Fairfax moved in the spring of 1649 to quash insubordination in the army, blamed on Leveller tracts that talked of 'new dictatorship' and asked the pointed question: 'We were before ruled by Kings, Lords and Commons; now by a General, Court Martial and House of Commons: and we pray you, what is the difference?' This fed the disaffection caused by war-weariness and impending service against the royalist forces in Ireland, and there was a mutinous outburst that Fairfax (against Cromwell's preference for mercy) crushed by having three of its leaders court-martialled and shot, outside the church at Burford where their followers were corralled. To prevent further disturbances from this 'enemy within', the Leveller pamphleteers were arrested and Lilburne was charged with treason. His trial – held in October 1649 – became one of the most important in legal history, because his inspired advocacy established a set of defendant's rights which would begin the process of turning the English criminal trial from a foregone conclusion into a genuine adversarial occasion, where the possibility of a 'not guilty' verdict was guaranteed by an independent jury.

Armed with Coke's *Institutes*, Lilburne disputed for three days with his judges, arguing quite literally for his life.[14] He was plainly guilty of the offence created by the new Treason Act, which punished by death any allegation that the government was unlawful: Lilburne had described it as an 'army junto' run by 'tyrants, weasels and polecats'. He knew that the army grandees wanted him dead and that the judges, notwithstanding the fair procedural rulings he had persuaded them to give, would in due course direct the jury to convict. He begged for an adjournment to relieve himself and collect his thoughts for his final speech. The judges ordered him to carry on, but Lilburne had one last precedent to create:

> Sir, if you will be so cruel as not to give me leave to withdraw to ease
> and refresh my body, I pray you let me do it in the court. Officer, I
> entreat you – help me to a chamber pot!

The judges sat in stunned silence as a chamber pot was fetched by the sheriff. Then, as the official transcript reports: 'When the pot came, he made water and gave it to the foreman,' who passed it around the jury. It was Lilburne's last and most important precedent: courts must ensure the comfort of the prisoners at the bar throughout their trial.

The judges directed the jury to convict, But it returned after an hour to acquit the defendant on all counts, to the noisy acclamation of Leveller supporters in the packed Guildhall. He was conveyed back to the Tower, by soldiers who joined in the shouts of joy at his deliverance, and it was a fortnight before the Council of State judged it safe to discharge him. His popularity was such that the government dared not move against him until 1651, when parliament held him in contempt for libelling an MP. By this device they denied him trial by jury and instead ordered him into exile on the continent. He returned in 1653, after Cromwell had dissolved 'the Rump', arguing plausibly that its dissolution had ended his liability for contempt of the House. He was arrested nonetheless, but his capacity to make legal history was undimmed. He invited the jury to pass judgement on the morality of the act of banishment rather than the more embarrassing factual question of whether he had breached it. The Statute had set the stakes too high by decreeing death should he return and the jury's verdict amounted to a condemnation of the MPs who passed it: 'John Lilburne is not guilty of any crime worthy of death.' There were the usual rejoicings in the street and amongst his guards, but the Council of State, in Star Chamber fashion, called each juror before it to demand an explanation. But the jurors had all met at the Windmill Tavern and agreed on their answer: 'I gave the verdict with a clear conscience and I refuse to answer any questions about it.'[15]

It was an unparalleled act of defiance. John Lilburne's juries had carved out a new role for that body as an independent protector of the citizen against the state. The Levellers had, finally, found one institution on which freeborn Englishmen could rely. Not the king, or parliament, or the army, but this protected body comprising twelve representatives of the people who would not be cowed or corrupted in their brief exercise of power over fellow citizens. It was the Leveller's' greatest achievement, through Lilburne's trials, to lodge in the English civil soul a sentimental attachment to trial by jury that no government ever after has been able to dislodge.

At Putney, their achievement was to advance a case for what Churchill came to describe as 'the worst form of government except for all the others'. It now appears in Article 21(1) and (3) of the Universal Declaration of Human Rights:

1. Everyone has the right to take part in the government of his country, directly or through freely chosen representatives.
3. The will of the people shall be the basis of the authority of government; this will shall be expressed in periodic and genuine elections which shall be by universal and equal suffrage and shall be held by secret vote or by equivalent free voting procedures.

The most remarkable feature of the last years of the twentieth century was the triumph of democracy as the central organizing principle for the nation state: most in Latin America have made the transition from military dictatorship, while one-party rule is diminishing in Africa and in

Asia and the USSR has splintered into a dozen crypto-democratic pieces. More countries within the Muslim tradition are turning to democratic elections – most notably Indonesia, but also (although with restrictions, especially upon women) Iran, Oman and Kuwait. Eighty-eight states are now accounted fully democratic, compared with fifty that are not and fifty-three that seem to be moving in a democratic direction. It would be wishful to think that dictators are a dying breed, but they are certainly in a defensive minority.[16]

It was under Cromwell, ironically, that alternatives were tried after 'the Rump' was ousted in 1653: a house of godly men ('Barebone's parliament') failed through lack of popular support; the *Instrument of Government*, a sound constitution that swept away rotten boroughs and provided for a presidential-style 'protectorship', was allowed to devolve into local military dictatorship by Major Generals. The death knell of the republic came from kingship cravings by its grand officers, who persuaded Cromwell to accept '*The Humble Petition and Advice*' which privileged him to appoint his successor: mimicking royalty, he chose his bumbling eldest son Richard. As if to prove that there is nothing in heredity, 'Tumbledown Dick' was no match for Charles II, although had Henry Ireton still been alive (he died of fever in Ireland in 1651) the Republic might well have been saved, or at least would have become an 'elective monarchy' of the kind suggested by Ireton in 'The Remonstrance' of 1648, doubtless with Henry IX the first to be elected. The Levellers continued to write, although Lilburne and Sexby died before the Restoration, the latter having been arrested not only for publishing a pamphlet urging death to dictators, but for making plans accordingly to kill Cromwell. Wildman lived to see the passage of the Bill of Rights of 1689, and ended his life, like so many on the English left ever after, as 'Sir' John. (He urged parliament to improve the calibre of voters by actually restricting the property franchise in land, from 40 shillings to £40!)

Some Leveller tracts were republished centuries later by the Chartists, over whom they had some influence, although in most modern socialist pantheons they have been eclipsed by 'true Levellers', i.e. the 'diggers' led to collective farming and reverberating hymn singing by Gerrard Winstanley. They were, however, much remembered in the UK 'underground' magazines in the '60s, whose editors were prosecuted and imprisoned for radical views on sex and drugs (*Oz* editor Richard Neville briefly cut a Lilburne-like figure at the Old Bailey) although further historical parallels fail when their messages are compared. They cannot even consistently be credited with republicanism: they left that to Ireton and his more dependable counsellors – Hugh Peters, John Cooke and John Milton, who derived their beliefs not from Leveller tracts (let alone from pagan Rome) but from the Bible, Magna Carta and 'Right Reason'. But the texts in this book show that it is the Levellers who most effortlessly leap history's hurdle to the present day, appearing to us not as promoters of any kind of 'ism' but as men who revel in fighting with their lives for free speech and free conscience, and who may by doing so be credited with expanding both human imagination and its permitted area of discourse. As Lilburne presciently put it, 'though we fail, our truths prosper'. Posterity has undoubtedly reaped the benefit of their dangerous endeavours.

SUGGESTED FURTHER READING

EDITIONS OF THE PUTNEY DEBATES:

Firth, C. H. (ed.), *The Clarke Papers*, volume 1, 1891 (reprinted with volume 2 as one volume, London, Royal Historical Society, 1992).

Woodhouse, A. S. P. (ed.), *Puritanism and Liberty*, London, J. M. Dent, 1938 (3rd edn 1986).

STUDIES OF THE PUTNEY DEBATES AND THE LEVELLERS:

Aylmer, G. E. (ed.), *The Levellers in the English Revolution*, London, Thames and Hudson, 1975.

Brailsford, H. N., *The Levellers and the English Revolution*, ed. Christopher Hill, 1961 (2nd edn, Nottingham, Spokesman, 1983).

Gregg, Pauline, *Free-Born John: A Biography of John Lilburne*, 1961 (reprinted London, Phoenix Press, 2000).

Hill, Christopher, *The World Turned Upside Down: Radical Ideas During the English Revolution*, London, Penguin, 1972.

Holstun, James, *Ehud's Dagger: Class Struggle in the English Revolution*, London and New York, Verso, 2000.

Mendle, Michael (ed.), *The Putney Debates of 1647*, Cambridge, Cambridge University Press, 2001.

Sharp, Andrew (ed.), *The English Levellers*, Cambridge, Cambridge University Press, 1998.

Woolrych, Austin, *Soldiers and Statesmen*, Oxford, Clarendon Press, 1987.

GLOSSARY

Agents: name referring to the small group of soldiers, principally drawn from five New Model horse regiments, who put their names to a series of pamphlets over the autumn of 1647, including 'The case of the army truly stated' and 'An agreement of the people'. During this time the agents were closely allied with civilians from London.

Agitators: name given to those officers and soldiers of the New Model who were selected to represent their respective regiments on the General Council of the Army.

Army engagements: as the New Model assumed an ever greater political role, it published a series of engagements, declarations and remonstrances in which it laid out its aims and objectives to the nation. Among the most important of these were the 'Solemn engagement' it entered into at Newmarket in June 1647 and the 'Declaration, or representation' which it endorsed on Triploe Heath in the same month.

General Council of the Army: an institution consisting of the general officers and two officer and two soldier representatives, or agitators, from each regiment of the New Model. Conceived in June 1647, it enabled the army's commanders to consult and include all ranks in the army's major political decisions. It was within the forum of the general council and its committees that the Putney debates took place.

Long Parliament: meet in November 1640 and continued to sit until its members were ejected by Cromwell in 1653. From the mid-1640s people on all sides of the civil war became increasingly critical of the assembly, attacking its authoritarian institutions and procedures, and its apparent desire to sit in perpetuity.

Negative voice: in the case of the crown, the power of the monarch to veto bills passed by both Houses of Parliament, thus preventing them from becoming law. In the case of the peerage, the power of the House of Lords to veto bills passed by the Commons, thus preventing their passage to the crown.

New Model Army: created by Parliament in 1645, it proved to be the decisive military force of the civil war. In June 1647 it refused to disband until Parliament redressed the grievances of both the soldiery and the people at large. However, the army gradually became a major political force in its own right, and eventually took it upon itself to settle the nation by purging Parliament and executing the king.

KEY FIGURES CITED IN THE TEXTS

Cromwell, Oliver (1599–1658): lieutenant-general of the New Model cavalry and Commons-man. He chaired the General Council on several days of the Putney debates, and was clearly shocked by the revolutionary concept underlying 'An agreement of the people'. One of the few individuals to side with Ireton during the debate on the franchise, he later forcefully denounced the 'Agreement' and its promoters. The sworn enemy of the Levellers by 1649, he twice unsuccessfully had Lilburne tried for his life.

Everard, Robert (*fl.*1647–1664): agent and trooper in Cromwell's regiment of horse. In the immediate days before the Putney debates he was the major go-between in discussions between the agents and members of the General Council. He attended and spoke boldly at the debates, but, being unknown to the clerks who recorded them, was identified and styled on the first day according to his distinctive 'buff coat', that is, a thick, short coat of leather.

Fairfax, Sir Thomas (1612–1671): captain-general and commander-in-chief of the New Model Army, and by July 1647 supreme commander of all Parliamentarian land forces in England and Wales. Despite his illustrious rank he seemingly played little part in the army's politicisation, although the soldiery continued to hold him in great esteem as their victorious military leader.

Ireton, Henry (1611–1651): commissary-general of the New Model horse, Commons-man and Cromwell's son-in-law. He was the most virulent opponent of 'An agreement of the people' at Putney, particularly of its clause on the franchise which he argued would lead to anarchy and the destruction of all property. This clearly placed him in a minority position among the debaters, as did his defence of the rights of the king and the lords in any future settlement.

Lilburne, John (1615–1657): 'Free-born John', leader of the Levellers. He was imprisoned by the bishops for distributing illicit puritan literature in the 1630s, and later fought for Parliament in the civil war. After leaving the army in 1645 he became a prolific pamphleteer and campaigner for religious and political liberty and the individual's rights at law. As a result he became a popular hero to many in London and the army, whilst successive governments ensured that he spent much of the remainder of his life either in prison or in exile.

Overton, Richard (*fl.*1640–1663): printer and pamphleteer. His early writings included a denial of the immortality of the soul and calls for religious liberty before he authored a number of works supporting Lilburne. He subsequently became a prominent Leveller and was perhaps their most effective propagandist in combining powerful invective with biting satire, as in his attack on Cromwell as the 'Great Bull of Bashan'.

Petty [or Pettus], Maximilian (*fl.*1617–1661): one of the two civilian delegates at Putney. By then he had been moving in army-civilian circles for some months, having attended the earlier discussions over 'The heads of the proposals'. At Putney he was outspoken in his condemnation of the negative voice of the king and the Lords, and his explanation of the franchise clause in 'An agreement of the people' was interpreted as a call for manhood suffrage. However, he later supported a compromise position that excluded apprentices, servants and almsmen from the vote.

Rainborough, Thomas (*d.*1648): colonel of a New Model foot regiment, Commons-man and briefly vice-admiral of the fleet. The most emotive and outspoken defender of manhood suffrage at Putney, he was probably also a committed republican. In November 1647 he was the highest ranking officer to support the ill-fated pro-'Agreement' army mutiny at Ware. His funeral in 1648 was turned into a mass Leveller demonstration at which mourners wore ribbons of his regimental colour, sea-green, which thereafter became the badge of Leveller allegiance.

Sexby, Edward (*d.*1658): agitator and trooper in Fairfax's regiment of horse. As one of the most active individuals in organising the army's initial defiance of Parliament, he was in close contact with civilians in London. He may have had a hand in 'The case of the army truly stated' and was clearly exceedingly close to the agents. At Putney he was the most outspoken critic of Cromwell and Ireton, displayed an obvious enmity towards the king and spoke powerfully on the behalf of the rights of the common soldier.

Walwyn, William (1600–1681): London merchant and pamphleteer. He was active on the city committees that supported the Parliamentarian war effort, and advocated religious liberty for all faiths in his first works. He later published in defence of Lilburne, became a leading Leveller and was perhaps their most radical thinker. In religion he seemingly believed in justification through faith alone, while in economics he wrote of the possibility (*pace* his fellow Levellers) of the community of goods and true, economic levelling if it were the universal desire of the people.

Wildman, John (1624–1693): the second civilian Putney debater. In the summer of 1647 he carried papers between London and the army and attended talks over 'The heads of the proposals'. He was possibly in early contact with the agents, may have contributed to 'The case of the army' and is the most likely author of the 'Agreement'. At Putney he was trenchant in his hostility to the 'Proposals', the negative voice of the king and the Lords, and the person of the king. In the aftermath of the debates he became deeply involved with Leveller agitation in London.

CHRONOLOGY

1646

24 June: Surrender of Oxford, the Royalist capital during the first civil war.

1647

5 June: New Model's 'Solemn engagement'.

14 June: New Model's 'Declaration, or representation'.

23 July: 'The heads of the proposals' submitted to the king.

18 October: 'The case of the army truly stated' presented to Fairfax.

28 October–11 November: The Putney debates.

15 November: Suppression of minor army mutiny in support of the 'Agreement'.

1648

March–August: Second civil war.

6 December: Army's purge of Parliament.

1649

30 January: Execution of Charles I.

28 March 1649: Arrest of Leveller leaders.

15 May: Crushing of significant pro-Leveller army mutiny at Burford.

26 October: Acquittal of Lilburne on charges of high treason.

NOTE ON TEXTS

With the exception of chapter 7, all the texts are based on original pamphlets in the British Library, London. Spelling, punctuation, capitalisation and dating have been modernised throughout, and a number of minor corrections and changes have silently been made.

The extracts from the Putney debates in chapter 7 are taken from the edition edited by A. S. P. Woodhouse in *Puritanism and Liberty* (3rd edn, London, J. M. Dent, 1986), with reference to the extract edited by David Wootton in *Divine Right and Democracy* (Harmondsworth, Penguin, 1986). A number of minor alterations and additions have silently been made in order to make the text more accessible.

I

A REMONSTRANCE OF MANY THOUSAND CITIZENS

July 1646

Appearing on London bookstalls in July 1646, the anti-monarchical content of 'A remonstrance of many thousand citizens' represented a counterblast to those calling for a speedy and lenient settlement with Charles I. Asserting the supremacy of the House of Commons over both the king and the Lords, this anonymous and inflammatory pamphlet is thought to be the work of the Leveller Richard Overton.[1]

A remonstrance of many thousand citizens and other freeborn people of England to their own House of Commons, occasioned through the illegal and barbarous imprisonment of that famous and worthy sufferer for his country's freedoms, Lieutenant-Colonel John Lilburne.[2] Wherein their just demands in behalf of themselves and the whole kingdom concerning their public safety, peace and freedom is expressed. Calling those their commissioners in Parliament[3] to an account: how they (since the beginning of their session to this present) have discharged their duties to the universality of the people, their sovereign lord, from whom their power and strength is derived, and by whom (*ad bene placitum*)[4] it is continued.

Printed in the year 1646.

We are well assured, yet cannot forget, that the cause of our choosing you to be Parliament-men was to deliver us from all kind of bondage and to preserve the commonwealth in peace and happiness. For effecting whereof we possessed you with the same power that was in ourselves to have done the same; for we might justly have done it ourselves without you if we had thought it convenient, choosing you (as persons whom we thought fitly qualified, and faithful) for avoiding some inconveniences. But you are to remember this was only of us but a power of trust (which is ever revocable, and cannot be otherwise) and to be employed to no other end than our own well-being. Nor did we choose you to continue our trusts longer than the known, established constitution of this commonwealth will justly permit, and that could be but for one year at the most: for by our law, a Parliament is to be called once every year, and oftener if need be,[5] as you well know. We are your principals, and you our agents; it is a truth you cannot but acknowledge. For if you or any other shall assume or exercise any power that is not derived from our trust and choice thereunto, that power is no less than usurpation and an oppression from which we expect to be freed, in whomsoever we find it – it being altogether inconsistent with the nature of just freedom, which you also very well understand.

The history of our forefathers since they were conquered by the Normans does manifest that this nation has been held in bondage all along ever since by the policies and force of the officers of trust in the commonwealth, amongst whom we always esteemed kings the chiefest. And what in much of the former time was done by war and by impoverishing of the people to make them slaves and to hold them in bondage, our latter princes have endeavoured to effect by giving ease and wealth unto the people; but withal corrupting their understanding by infusing false principles concerning kings and governments and Parliaments and freedoms, and also using all means to corrupt and vitiate the manners of the youth, and the strongest prop and support of the people, the gentry.

It is wonderful[6] that the failings of former kings to bring our forefathers into bondage (together with the trouble and danger that some of them drew upon themselves and their posterity by those their unjust endeavours) had not wrought in our latter kings a resolution to rely on and trust only to justice and square dealing with the people, especially considering the unaptness of the nation to bear much, especially from those that pretend to love them and unto whom they expressed so much hearty affection (as any people in the world ever did) as in the quiet admission of King James from Scotland[7] – sufficient (if any obligation would work kings to reason) to have endeared both him and his son King Charles to an inviolable love and hearty affection to the English nation. But it would not do.

They chose rather to trust unto their policies and court arts, to king-waste and delusion, than to justice and plain dealing, and did effect many things tending to our enslaving (as in your first remonstrance[8] you show skill enough to manifest the same to all the world). And this nation, having been by their delusive arts and a long-continued peace much softened and debased in judgement and spirit, did bear far beyond its usual temper or any example of our forefathers, which (to our shame), we acknowledge.

But, in conclusion, longer they would not bear; and then you were chosen to work our deliverance and to instate us in natural and just liberty agreeable to reason and common equity. For whatever our forefathers were, or whatever they did or suffered or were enforced to yield unto, we are the men of the present age and ought to be absolutely free from all kinds of exorbitances, molestations or arbitrary power; and you we chose to free us from all, without exception or limitation either in respect of persons, officers, degrees or things. And we were full of confidence that you also would have dealt impartially on our behalf and made us the most absolute free people in the world.

But how you have dealt with us we shall now let you know; and let the righteous God judge between you and us. The continual oppressors of the nation have been kings, which is so evident that you cannot deny it. And you yourselves have told the king (whom yet you own) that his whole 16 years' reign was one continued act of the breach of the law. You showed him that you understood his under-working with Ireland, his endeavour to enforce the Parliament by the army raised against Scotland.[9] You were eye-witnesses of his violent attempt about the five members;[10] you saw evidently his purpose of raising war; you have seen him engaged, and with obstinate violence persisting in the most bloody war that ever this nation knew, to the wasting and destruction of multitudes of honest and religious people. You have experience that none but a king could do so great intolerable mischiefs; the very name of 'king' proving a sufficient charm to delude many of our brethren in Wales, Ireland, England and Scotland too, so far as to fight against their own liberties, which you know no man under heaven could ever have done.

And yet – as if you were of counsel with him and were resolved to hold up his reputation, thereby to enable him to go on in mischief – you maintained 'The king can do no wrong', and applied all his oppressions to evil counsellors, begging and entreating him in such submissive language to return to his kingly office and Parliament as if you were resolved to make us believe he were a god without whose presence all must fall to ruin, or as if it were impossible for any nation to be happy without a king. You cannot fight for our liberties, but it must be in the name of king and Parliament; he that speaks of his cruelties must be thrust out of your House and society; your preachers must pray for him, as if he had not deserved to be excommunicated by all Christian society, or as if you or they thought God were a respecter of the persons of kings in judgement.

By this and other your like dealings – your frequent treating and tampering to maintain his honour – we that have trusted you to deliver us from his oppressions and to preserve us from his cruelties are wasted and consumed in multitudes to manifold miseries, whilst you lie ready with open arms to receive him and to make him a great and glorious king.

Have you shaken this nation like an earthquake to produce no more than this for us? Is it for this that you have made so free use and been so bold both with our persons and estates? And do you (because of our readiness to comply with your desires in all things) conceive us so sottish[11] as to be contented with such unworthy returns of our trust and love? No. It is high time we be plain with you. We are not, nor shall not be so contented. We do expect according to reason that you should in the first place declare and set forth King Charles his wickedness openly before the world, and withal to show the intolerable inconveniences of having a kingly government from the constant evil practices of those of this nation, and so to declare King Charles an enemy, and to publish your resolution never to have any more to do with him, but to acquit us of so great a charge and trouble forever and to convert the great revenue of the crown to the public treasure to make good the injuries and injustices done heretofore, and of late, by those that have possessed the same. And this we expected long since at your hand; and until this be done we shall not think ourselves well dealt withal in this original of all oppressions, to wit kings.

You must also deal better with us concerning the Lords than you have done. You only are chosen by us the people; and therefore in you only is the power of binding the whole nation by making, altering or abolishing of laws. You have therefore prejudiced us in acting so as if you could not make a law without both the royal assent of the king (so you are pleased to express yourselves) and the assent of the Lords; yet when either king or

Lords assent not to what you approve, you have so much sense of your own power as to assent what you think good by an order of your own House.

What is this but to blind our eyes, that we should not know where our power is lodged, nor to whom to apply ourselves for the use thereof? But if we want a law, we must wait till the king and Lords assent; if an ordinance, then we must wait till the Lords assent. Yet you, knowing their assent to be merely formal (as having no root in the choice of the people, from whom the power that is just must be derived), do frequently importune their assent, which implies a most gross absurdity. For where their assent is necessary and essential, they must be as free as you to assent or dissent as their understandings and consciences should guide them and might as justly importune you as you them. You ought in conscience to reduce this case also to a certainty, and not to waste time, and open your counsels, and be liable to so many obstructions as you have been. Prevail with them (enjoying their honours and possessions) to be liable and stand to be chosen for knights and burgesses by the people as other the gentry and free-men of this nation do, which will be an obligation upon them as having one and the same interest; then also they would be distinguished by their virtues and love to the commonwealth, whereas now they act and vote in our affairs but as intruders or as thrust upon us by kings to make good their interests, which to this day have been to bring us into a slavish subjection to their wills.

Nor is there any reason that they should in any measure be less liable to any law than the gentry are. Why should any of them assault, strike or beat any, and not be liable to the law as other men are? Why should not they be as liable to their debts as other men?[12] There is no reason: yet have you stood still and seen many of us, and some of yourselves, violently abused without reparation.

We desire you to free us from these abuses and their negative voices,[13] or else tell us that it is reasonable we should be slaves, this being a perpetual prejudice in our government neither consulting with freedom nor safety. With freedom it cannot: for in this way of voting in all affairs of the commonwealth, being not chosen thereunto by the people, they are therein masters and lords of the people, which necessarily implies the people to be their servants and vassals. And they have used many of us accordingly, by committing divers to prison upon their own authority, namely William Larner,[14] Lieutenant-Colonel John Lilburne and other worthy sufferers, who upon appeal unto you have not been relieved.

We must therefore pray you to make a law against all kinds of arbitrary government as the highest capital offence against the commonwealth, and to reduce all conditions of men to a certainty, that none henceforward may presume or plead anything in way of excuse, and that you will have no favour or scruple of tyrannical power over us in any whatsoever.

Time has revealed hidden things unto us, things covered over thick and threefold with pretences of the true reformed religion, when as we see apparently that this nation and that of Scotland are joined together in a most bloody and consuming war by the waste and policy of a sort of lords in each nation that were malcontents and vexed that the king had advanced others, and not themselves, to the managing of state affairs. Which they suffered till the king, increasing his oppressions in both nations, gave them opportunity to reveal themselves; and then they resolved to bring the king to their bow and regulation, and to exclude all those from managing state affairs that he had advanced thereunto, and who were grown so insolent and presumptuous as these discontented ones were liable to continual molestations from them, either by practices at Council Table, High Commission or Star Chamber.[15]

So their work was to subvert the monarchical lords and clergy, and therewithal to abate the power of the king, and to order him. But this was a mighty work and they were nowise able to effect it of themselves. 'Therefore' (say they) 'the generality of the people must be engaged; and how must this be done?' 'Why' (say they) 'we must associate with that part of the clergy that are now made underlings and others of them that have been oppressed, and with the most zealous religious nonconformists; and by the help of these we will lay before the generality of the people all the popish innovations in religion, all the oppressions of the bishops and High Commission, all the exorbitances of the Council Board and Star Chamber, all the injustice of the Chancery and courts of justice, all the illegal taxations (as ship money,[16] patents and projects) whereby we shall be sure to get into our party the generality of the City of London and all the considerable substantial people of both nations – by whose cry and importunity we shall have a Parliament, which we shall by our manifold ways, alliances, dependants and relations soon work to our purposes.'

'But' (say some) 'this will never be affected without a war; for the king will have a strong party and he will never submit to us.' ''Tis not expected otherwise' (say they); 'and great and vast sums of money must be raised, and soldiers and ammunition must be had, whereof we shall not need to fear any want. For what will not an oppressed, rich and religious people do to be delivered from all kinds of oppression, both spiritual and temporal, and to be restored to purity and freedom in religion, and to the just liberty of their persons and estates? All our care must be to hold all at our command and disposing. For if this people thus stirred up by us should make an end too soon with the king and his party, it is not much to be doubted they would place the supreme power in their House of Commons, unto whom only of right it belongs – they only being chosen by the people, which is so presently discerned that as we have a care the king and his lords must not prevail, so more especially we must be careful the supreme power fall not into the people's hands, or House of Commons'.'

'Therefore we must so act as not to make an end with the king and his party, till, by expense of time and treasure, a long, bloody and consuming war, decay of trade and multitudes of the highest impositions, the people by degrees are tired and wearied, so as they shall not be able to contest or dispute with us either about supreme or inferior power. But we will be able, before they are aware, to give them both law and religion.'

'In Scotland it will be easy to establish the Presbyterian government in the church; and that being once effected, it will not be much difficult in England, upon a pretence of uniformity in both nations and the like, unto which there will be found a clergy as willing as we, it giving them as absolute a ministry over the consciences of the people, over their persons and purses, as we ourselves aim at, or desire. And if any shall presume to oppose either us or them, we shall be easily able by the help of the clergy, by our party in the House of Commons and by their and our influence in all parts of both nations, easily to crush and suppress them.'

'Well' (say some), 'all this may be done; but we, without abundance of travail[17] to ourselves and wounding our own consciences (for we must grossly dissemble before God, and all the world will see it in time), we can never do all this that you aim at but by the very same oppressions as were practised by the king, the bishops and all those his tyrannical instruments both in religion and civil government. And it will never last or continue long: the people will see it and hate you for it, more than ever they hated the former tyrants and oppressors. Were it not better and safer for us to be just, and really to do that for the people which we pretend and for which we shall so freely spend their lives and estates, and so have their love, and enjoy the peace of quiet consciences?'

'But' (say some) 'are not we a lord, a peer of the kingdom? Have you your lordship or peerage, or those honours and privileges that belong thereunto from the love and election of the people? Your interest is as different from theirs and as inconsistent with their freedoms as those lords' and clergy's are whom we strive to supplant. And therefore rather than satisfy the people's expectations in what concerns their freedoms, it were much better to continue as we are and never disturb the king in his prerogatives nor his lords and prelates in their privileges. And therefore let us be as one; and when we talk of conscience, let us make conscience to make good unto ourselves and our posterities those dignities, honours and pre-eminencies conveyed unto us by our noble progenitors by all the means we can, not making questions for conscience' sake, or any other things. And if we be united in our endeavours, and work wisely, observing when to advance and when to give ground, we cannot fail of success, which will be an honour to our names for ever.'

These are the strong delusions that have been amongst us; and the mystery of iniquity[18] has wrought most vehemently in all our affairs. Hence it was that Strafford was so long in trial[19] and that he had no greater heads to bear his company. Hence it was: that the king was not called to an account for his oppressive government, and that the treachery of those that would have enforced you was not severely punished; that the king gained time to raise an army, and the queen to furnish ammunition; that our first and second armies were so ill formed, and as ill managed. Sherburn, Brentford, Exeter, the slender use of the Associate Counties, the slight guarding of the sea, Oxford, Dennington, the west defeat,[20] did all proceed from (and upon) the mystery of iniquity.

The king and his party had been nothing in your hands had not some of you been engaged, and some of you ensnared, and the rest of you overborne with this mystery, which you may now easily perceive if you have a mind thereunto. That you were put upon the continuation of this Parliament during the pleasure of both Houses was from this mystery, because in time these politicians had hopes to work and pervert you to forsake the common interest of those that chose and trusted you, to promote their unjust design to enslave us, wherein they have prevailed too, too, much.

For we must deal plainly with you: you have long time acted more like the House of Peers than the House of Commons. We can scarcely approach your door with a request or motion, though by way of petition, but you hold long debates whether we break not your privileges. The king's or the Lords' pretended prerogatives never made a greater noise nor was made more dreadful than the name of privilege of the House of Commons.

Your members, in all impositions, must not be taxed in the places where they live, like other men. Your servants have their privileges too. To accuse or prosecute any of you is become dangerous to the prosecutors. You have imprisonments as frequent for either witnesses or prosecutors as ever the Star Chamber had, and you are furnished with new-devised arguments to prove that you only may justly do these gross injustices which the Star Chamber, High Commission and Council Board might not do, and for doing whereof (whilst you were untainted) you abolished them. But you now frequently commit men's persons to prison without showing cause. You examine men upon interrogatories and questions against themselves, and imprison them for refusing to answer;[21] and you have officious servile men that write and publish sophistical arguments to justify your so doing, for which they are rewarded and countenanced, as the Star Chamber and High Commission beagles lately were, whilst those that ventured their lives for your establishment are many of them vexed and molested and impoverished by them. You have entertained to be your committees' servants those very prowling varlets that were employed by those unjust courts who took pleasure to torment honest conscionable people. You vex and molest honest men for matters of religion and difference with you and your Synod in judgement, and take upon you to determine of doctrine and discipline (approving this, and reproaching that, just like unto former ignorant politic and superstitious Parliaments and convocations) and thereby have divided honest people amongst themselves by countenancing only those of the presbytery and discountenancing all the Separation, Anabaptists and Independents.

And though it rests in you to quiet all differences in affection, though not in judgement, by permitting everyone to be fully persuaded in their own minds, commanding all reproach to cease, yet as you also had admitted Machiavelli's maxim '*Divide et impera*', 'divide and prevail', you countenance only one, open the printing press only unto one, and that to the presbytery, and suffer them to rail and abuse and domineer over all the rest – as if also you had discovered and digested that without a powerful, compulsive presbytery in the church, a compulsive mastership or aristocratical government over the people in the state could never long be maintained.

Whereas truly we are well assured, neither you nor none else can have any power at all to conclude the people in matters that concern the worship of God. For therein every one of us ought to be fully assured in our own minds and to be sure to worship Him according to our consciences. You may propose what form you conceive best and most available for information and well-being of the nation, and may persuade and invite thereunto; but compel, you cannot justly. For you have no power from us so to do, nor could you have. For we could not confer a power that was not in ourselves, there being none of us that can without wilful sin bind ourselves to worship God after any other way than what (to a tittle) in our own particular understandings we approve to be just. And therefore we could not refer ourselves to you in things of this nature. And surely if we could not confer this power upon you, you cannot have it, and so not exercise it justly. No, as we ought not to revile or reproach any man for his differing with us in judgement more than we would be reviled or reproached for ours, even so you ought not to countenance any reproachers or revilers or molesters for matters of conscience but to protect and defend all that live peaceably in the commonwealth, of what judgement or way of worship whatsoever.

And if you would bend your minds thereunto and leave yourselves open to give ear and to consider such things as would be presented unto you, a just way would be discovered for the peace and quiet of the land in general and of every well-minded person in particular. But if you lock up yourselves from hearing all voices, how is it possible you should try all things? It is not for you to assume a power to control and force religion or a way of church government upon the people because former Parliaments have so done. You are first to prove that you could have such a power justly entrusted unto you by the people that trusted you, which you see you have not.

We may haply be answered that the king's writ that summons a Parliament and directs the people to choose knights and burgesses implies the establishment of religion. To which we answer that if kings would prove themselves lawful magistrates they must prove themselves to be so by a lawful derivation of their authority, which must be from the voluntary trust of the people; and then the case is the same with them as between the people and you, they (as you) being possessed of no more power than what is in the people justly to entrust. And then all implications in the writs of the establishment of religion show that in that particular, as many other, we remain under the Norman yoke of an unlawful power, from which we ought to free ourselves, and which you ought not to maintain upon us, but to abrogate.

But you have listened to any counsels rather than to the voice of us that trusted you. Why is it that you have stopped the press but that you would have nothing but pleasing, flattering discourses and go on to make yourselves partakers of the lordship over us, without hearing anything to the contrary?

Yes, your lords and clergy long to have us in the same condition with our deluded brethren, the commons of Scotland, where their understandings are so captivated with a reverend opinion of their presbytery that they really believe them to be by divine authority, and are as zealous therein as ever the poor deceived papists were. As much they live in fear of their thunder-bolts of excommunication – and good cause they have, poor souls, for those excommunications are so followed with the civil sanction, or secular power – that they are able to crush any opposer or dissenter to dust, to undo or ruin any man. So absolute a power has their new clergy already gained over the poor people there, and earnestly labour to bring us into the same condition, because if we should live in greater freedom in this nation it would (they know) in time be observed by their people, whose understandings would be thereby informed, and then they would grow impatient of their thraldom and shake off their yoke.

They are also in no less bondage in things civil. The lords and great men over-rule all as they please; the people are scarce free in anything.

Friends, these are known truths.

And hence it is that in their counsels here they adhere to those that maintain their own greatness and usurped rule over us, lest if we should here possess greater liberty than their vassals, the people in Scotland, they might in short time observe the same and discharge themselves of their oppressions.

It is from the mystery of iniquity that you have never made that use of the people of this nation in your war as you might have done, but have chosen rather to hazard their coming in than to arm your own native undoubted friends; by which means they are possessed of too many considerable strengths of this nation, and speak such language in their late published papers as if they were not paid for their slow assistance. Whereas you might have ended the war long before, if by sea or land you had showed yourselves resolved to make us a free people. But it is evident a change of our bondage is the uttermost is intended us, and that, too, for a worse, and longer, if we shall be so contented.

But it is strange you should imagine that. The truth is we find none are so much hated by you as those you think do discern those your purposes, or that apply themselves unto you with motions tending to divert you from proceeding therein. For some years now, no condition of men can prevail with you to amend anything that is amiss in the commonwealth.

The exorbitances in the City's government and the strivings about prerogatives in the mayor and aldermen against the freedoms of the commons (and to their extreme prejudice) are returned to the same point they were at in Garway's time,[22] which you observe, and move not, nor assist the commons. No, worse than in his time, they are justified by the mayor in a book published and sent by him to every common councilman.

The oppression of the Turkey Company and the Adventurers' Company, and all other infringements of our native liberties of the same nature[23] and which in the beginnings of the Parliament you seemed to abominate, are now by you complied withal and licensed to go on in their oppressions.

You know the laws of this nation are unworthy a free people and deserve from first to last to be considered and seriously debated, and reduced to an agreement with common equity and right reason, which ought to be the form and life of every government – Magna Carta itself being but a beggarly thing containing many marks of intolerable bondage; and the laws that have been made since by Parliaments have in very many particulars made our government much more oppressive and intolerable.

The Norman way for ending of controversies was much more abusive than the English way; yet the Conqueror, contrary to his oath, introduced the Norman laws and his litigious and vexatious way amongst us. The like he did also for punishment of malefactors, controversies of all natures having before a quick and final dispatch in every hundred. He erected a trade of judges and lawyers to sell justice and injustice at his own unconscionable rate and in what time he pleased, the corruption whereof is yet remaining upon us to our continual impoverishing and molestation from which we thought you should have delivered us.

You know also imprisonment for debt is not from the beginning. Yet you think not of those many thousand persons and families that are destroyed thereby. You are rich and abound in goods and have need of nothing; but the afflictions of the poor, your hunger-starved brethren, you have no compassion of. Your zeal makes a noise as far as Argiere to deliver those captive Christians at the charge of others,[24] but those whom your own unjust laws hold captive in your own prisons, these are too near you to think of. No, you suffer poor Christians, for whom Christ died, to kneel before you in the streets, aged, sick and crippled, begging your half-penny charities, and you rustle by them in your coaches and silks daily, without regard or taking any course for their constant relief. Their sight would melt the heart of any Christian and yet it moves not you nor your clergy.

We entreat you to consider what difference there is between binding a man to an oar as a galley-slave in Turkey or Argiere, and pressing of men to serve in your war. To surprise a man on the sudden, force him from his calling where he lived comfortably from a good trade, from his dear parents, wife or children, against inclination and disposition to fight for a cause he understands not and in company of such as he has no comfort to be withal, for pay that will scarce give him sustenance – and if he live, to return to a lost trade, or beggary, or not much better: if any tyranny or cruelty exceed this, it must be worse than that of a Turkish galley-slave.

But you are apt to say, 'What remedy? Men we must have.' To which we answer in behalf of ourselves and our too-much-injured brethren that are pressed, that the Hollanders, our provident neighbours, have no such cruelties, esteeming nothing more unjust or unreasonable; yet they want no men. And if you would take care that all sorts of men might find comfort and contentment in your government, you would not need to enforce men to serve your wars. And if you would in many things follow their good example and make this nation a state free from the oppression of kings and the corruptions of the court and show love to the people in the constitutions of your government, the affection of the people would satisfy all common and public occasions. And in many particulars we can show you a remedy for this and all other inconveniences, if we could find you inclined to hear us.

You are extremely altered in demeanour towards us. In the beginning you seemed to know what freedom was, made a distinction of honest men, whether rich or poor. All were welcome to you, and you would mix yourselves with us in a loving familiar way, void of courtly observance or behaviour. You kept your committee doors open; all might hear and judge of your dealings. Hardly you would permit men to stand bare-headed before you, some of you telling them you more regarded their health, and that they should not deem[25] of you as of other domineering courts. You and they were one, all commons of England. And the like ingenious carriage by which you won our affections to that height that you no sooner demanded anything but it was effected. You did well then. Who did hinder you? The mystery of iniquity: that was it that perverted your course.

What a multitude of precious lives have been lost? What a mass of monies have been raised? What one way was proposed to advance monies that was refused by you, though never so prejudicial to the people?; allowing your committees to force men to pay or lend or else to swear that they were not worth so or so: the most destructive course to tradesmen that could be devised, fifty entire subsidies to be lent throughout London, if not procured, yet authorised by you. Never the like heard of. And the excise, that being once settled, all other assessments should cease.[26] Notwithstanding, in few months comes forth ordinance upon ordinance for more monies. And for the customs: they were thought an oppression in the beginning, and being so high, an hindrance to trade and extremely prejudicial to the nation. Nevertheless, they are now confirmed with many augmentations, in so much as men of inferior trading find great trouble to provide monies for customs and have so many officers to please that it is a very slavery to have anything to do with them; and no remedy, the first commissioners being more harsh and ingenious than the late farmers, and the last worse then the former.

Truly it is a sad thing but too true: a plain, quiet-minded man in any place in England is just like a harmless sheep in a thicket – can hardly move or stir but he shall be stretched and lose his wool. Such committees have you made in all cities and counties, and none are so ill-used as honest godly men.

You have now sat full five years, which is four years longer than we intended; for we could choose you but for (at most) one year. And now we wish you would publish to all the world the good that you have done for us, the liberty you have brought us unto. If you could excuse yourselves as you used to do by saying it has been a time of war, that will not do. For when the war might in the beginning have been prevented if you had drawn a little more blood from the right vein, and might often (before this) have been ended, occasion has been given away and treated away. And now, when through the faithfulness of the New Model[27] you have almost forced an end and have no great part to effect, now again at the instigation of those that love their kings more than all this nation and their own, his sacred or holy majesty must again be treated with; their national and Solemn League and Covenant with their God binding them to be respecters of persons in judgement and to preserve his person in the defence of the true, Protestant religion and liberty of the people[28] that has constantly against all persuasion and obligation done whatever he could to subvert both. If this be not the height of the mystery of iniquity, what is higher?

But let not these be deceived, nor thus under zealous expressions deceive you. We wish your souls may no further enter into their secret; for God will not be mocked nor suffer such gross hypocrisy to pass without exemplary punishment. And if you believe there is a God, you must believe it; and if you do believe it, and consider the ways you have trod and truly repent, show it by walking contrary to what you have done or purposed to do and let us quickly and speedily partake thereof. For God is a God that takes vengeance and will not suffer you to go on to our ruin.

We have some hopes you will; for amongst you there have been always faithful and worthy men whose abundant grief it has been to observe the strange progress of the chosen men of the commonwealth, and have strove exceedingly on all occasions to produce better effects, and some Christians of late produced to their praise.

Others there are that have been only misled by the policies and stratagems of politic men; and these, after this our serious advice, will make you more seriously study the common interest of this nation. Others there are, and those a great number, that are newly chosen into your House, and we trust are such as will exceedingly strengthen the good part that hitherto has been too weak to steer an even course amidst so many oppositions and cross waves, but henceforth joined all in one will be able to do and carry on whatsoever is just and good for the commonwealth, the more just and good, the more easily effected; for such things are easily to be made evident to all men and can never fail of the uttermost assistance of all well-minded people.

And therefore we would not have you to be discouraged in attempting whatsoever is evidently just. For we will therein assist you to the last drop of our blood. Fear neither the Anakims nor the sons of the giants:[29] for the Lord our God He will stand by you in all things that are just and will bless and prosper you therein.

Forsake and utterly renounce all crafty and subtle intentions; hide not your thoughts from us and give us encouragement to be open-breasted unto you. Proclaim beforehand what you determine to do in establishing anything for continuance, and hear all things that can be spoken with or against the same. And to that intent, let the imprisoned presses at liberty that all men's understandings may be more conveniently informed and convinced as far as is possible by the equity of your proceedings.

We cannot but expect to be delivered from the Norman bondage whereof we now as well as our predecessors have felt the smart by these bloody wars, and from all unreasonable laws made ever since that unhappy conquest. As we have encouragement, we shall inform you further, and guide you as we observe your doings.

The work, you must note, is ours and not your own, though you are to be partakers with us in the well or ill-doing thereof. And therefore you must expect to hear more frequently from us than you have done; nor will it be your wisdom to take these admonitions and cautions in evil part. If you consider well you may wonder we are no tarter. You may perceive we have not yet left our true English confidence, but are willing that both you and all our neighbour nations should know that we both see and know all stratagems and policies that are laid in wait to entrap (and so to enslave) us, and that we bid defiance to their worst our enemies can do. We know we have store of friends in our neighbour countries.

Our head is not yet so intoxicated with this new mystery of iniquity but that a reasonable cordial administered by your hand will set us fast in our seat.

You are not to reckon that you have any longer time to effect the great work we have entrusted unto you; for we must not lose our free choice of a Parliament once every year, fresh and fresh for a continual Parliament. For so, if a present Parliament be mistaken in their understandings and do things prejudicial, we may so long remain under these prejudices that the commonwealth may be endangered thereby. Nor do we value a triennial Parliament; before three years come to an end, grievances and mischiefs may be past remedy.

And therefore our advice is that you order a meeting of the choosing of Parliament-men to be expressly upon one certain day in November yearly throughout the land in the places accustomed and to be by you expressed, there to make choice of whom they think good, according to law, and all men that have a right to be there, not to fail upon a great penalty, but no summons to be expected. And if any person without exception shall write letters or use any endeavours to incline the choosers to choose any man, or use any means to disturb or pervert them from a free choice, then that all such sinister dealing be made punishable or a most heinous crime.

And that a Parliament so chosen in November, succeeding year by year, may come in stead of the preceding Parliament, and proceed with the affairs of the commonwealth. Nor would we have it in the power of our Parliament to remove any member from his place or service of the House without the consent had of those counties, cities and boroughs respectively that choose him; great inconveniences depending thereon, whereof we have seen and felt too much.

Now, if you shall conscionably perform your trust the year ensuing and order the Parliaments to succeed as aforesaid, then we shall not doubt to be made absolute free-men in time, and become a just, plenteous and powerful nation. All that is past will be forgotten and we shall yet have cause to rejoice in your wisdom and fidelity.

POSTSCRIPT

Moreover, as for me, God forbid that I should sin against the Lord in ceasing to pray for you: but I will teach you the good and the right way. Only fear the Lord and serve him in truth and with all your heart: for consider how great things he has done for you. But if you shall still do wickedly, you shall be consumed, both you and your king. 1 Samuel 22: 23–25.

FINIS.

2

THE LARGE PETITION

March 1647

In March 1647 a copy of the 'large', that is, comprehensive petition was seized in London while being circulated for subscription. With its bold and revolutionary claim that the Commons was the supreme authority of the nation, it caused considerable uproar within Parliament. Two of its promoters were imprisoned and the petition itself was burned by the common hangman. Known to be a collaborative work, the Leveller William Walwyn[1] was prominent amongst its authors.

To the right honourable and supreme authority of this nation, the Commons in Parliament assembled. The humble petition of many thousands, earnestly desiring the glory of God, the freedom of the commonwealth and the peace of all men.

Shows,
That as no government is more just in the constitution than that of Parliaments, having its foundation in the free choice of the people, and as the end of all government is the safety and freedom of the governed, even so the people of this nation in all times have manifested most hearty affection unto Parliaments as the most proper remedy of their grievances. Yet such have been the wicked policies of those who from time to time have endeavoured to bring this nation into bondage that they have in all times, either by the disuse or abuse of Parliaments, deprived the people of their hopes. For testimony whereof the late times foregoing this Parliament will sadly witness: when it was not only made a crime to mention a Parliament, but either the pretended negative voice (the most destructive to freedom) or a speedy dissolution[2] blasted the fruit and benefit thereof, whilst the whole land was overspread with all kinds of oppression and

tyranny extending both to soul and body, and that in so rooted and settled a way that the complaints of the people in general witnessed that they would have given anything in the world for one six months' freedom of Parliament. Which has been since evidenced in their instant and constant readiness of assistance to this present Parliament, exceeding the records of all former ages, and wherein God has blessed them with their first desires, making this Parliament the most absolute and free of any Parliament that ever was, and enabling it with power sufficient to deliver the whole nation from all kinds of oppressions and grievances, though of never so long continuance, and to make it the most absolute and free nation in the world.

And it is most thankfully acknowledged that you have in order to the freedom of the people suppressed the High Commission, Star Chamber and Council Table; called home the banished,[3] delivered such as were imprisoned for matters of conscience[4] and brought some delinquents to deserved punishment;[5] that you have suppressed the bishops and popish lords, abolished episcopacy and that kind of prelatic persecuting government;[6] that you have taken away ship money and all the new illegal patents. Whereby the hearts of all the well-affected were enlarged and filled with a confident hope that they should have seen long before this a complete removal of all grievances, and the whole people delivered from all oppressions over soul or body.

But such is our misery, that after the expense of so much precious time, of blood, and treasure, and the ruin of so many thousands of honest families in recovering our liberties, we still find this nation oppressed with grievances of the same destructive nature as formerly, though under other notions; and which are so much the more grievous unto us because they are inflicted in the very time of this present Parliament, under God, the hope of the oppressed. For, as then all the men and women in England were made liable to the summons, attachments, sentences and imprisonments of the lords of the Council Board, so we find by woeful experience and sufferings of many particular persons that the present lords do assume and exercise the same power, than which nothing is, or can be, more repugnant and destructive to the commons' just liberties.

As the unjust power of Star Chamber was exercised in compelling of men and women to answer to interrogatories tending to accuse themselves and others, so is the same now frequently practised upon divers persons – even your cordial friends, that have been, and still are, punished for refusing to answer to questions against themselves and nearest relations.

As then the great oppression of the High Commission was most evident in molesting of godly peaceable people for nonconformity or different opinion and practice in religion, judging all who were contrary-minded to themselves to be heretics, sectaries, schismatics, seditious, factious enemies to the state, and the like; and under great penalties forbidding all persons not licensed by them to preach or publish the gospel – even so now at this day, the very same if not greater molestations are set on foot and violently prosecuted by the instigation of a clergy no more infallible than the former, to the extreme discouragement and affliction of many thousands of your faithful adherents, who are not satisfied that controversies in religion can be trusted to the compulsive regulation of any, and after the bishops were suppressed, did hope never to have seen such a power assumed by any in this nation any more.

And although all new illegal patents are by you abolished, yet the oppressive monopoly of Merchant Adventurers and others do still remain to the great abridgement of the liberties of the people and to the extreme prejudice of all such industrious people as depend on clothing or other woollen manufacture (it being the staple commodity of this nation), and to the great discouragement and disadvantage of all sorts of tradesmen, seafaring men, and hindrance of shipping and navigation.

Also the old tedious and chargeable way of deciding controversies or suits in law is continued to this day, to the extreme vexation and utter undoing of multitudes of families, a grievance as great and as palpable as any in the world. Likewise that old but most unequal punishment of malefactors is still continued, whereby men's lives and liberties are as liable to the law, and corporal pains as much inflicted for small as for great offences, and that most unjustly upon the testimony of one witness, contrary both to the law of God and common equity: a grievance very great but little regarded.

Also tithes[7] and other enforced maintenance are still continued, though there be no ground for either under the gospel and though the same have occasioned multitudes of suits, quarrels and debates, both in former and later times. In like manner, multitudes of poor distressed prisoners for debt lie still unregarded in a most miserable and woeful condition throughout the land, to the great reproach of this nation. Likewise prison-keepers or gaolers are as presumptuous as ever they were, both in receiving and detaining of prisoners illegally committed; as cruel and inhumane to all, especially to such as are well-affected; as oppressive and extorting in their fees, and are attended with under-officers of such vile and unchristian demeanour as is most abominable. Also thousands of men and women are still (as formerly) permitted to live in beggary and wickedness all their life long and to breed their children to the same idle and vicious course of life, and no effectual means used to reclaim either or to reduce them to any virtue or industry.

And last, as those who found themselves aggrieved formerly at the burdens and oppressions of those times (that did not conform to the church government then established, refused to pay ship money or yield obedience to unjust patents) were reviled and reproached with nick-names of Puritans, heretics, schismatics, sectaries, or were termed factious or seditious, men of turbulent spirits, despisers of government and disturbers of the public peace; even so is it at this day in all respects, with those who show any sensibility of the fore-recited grievances, or move in any manner or measure for remedy thereof; all the reproaches, evils and mischiefs that can be devised are thought too few or too little to be laid upon them, as Roundheads, sectaries, Independents, heretics, schismatics, factious, seditious, rebellious, disturbers of the public peace, destroyers of all civil relation and subordinations. Yes, and beyond what was formerly, nonconformity is now judged a sufficient cause to disable any person, though of known fidelity, from bearing any office of trust in the commonwealth,[8] whilst neuters, malignants and disaffected are admitted and continued.[9] And though it be not now made a crime to mention a Parliament, yet is it little less to mention the supreme power of this honourable House.

So that in all these respects this nation remains in a very sad and disconsolate condition; and the more, because it is thus with us after so long a session of so powerful and so free a Parliament, and which has been so made and maintained by the abundant love and liberal effusion of the blood of the people.

And therefore, knowing no danger nor thraldom like unto our being left in this most sad condition by this Parliament, and observing that you are now drawing the great and weighty affairs of this nation to some kind of conclusion, and fearing that you may before long be obstructed by something equally evil to a negative voice, and that you may be induced to lay by that strength which (under God) has hitherto made you powerful to all good works;[10] whilst we have yet time to hope, and you power to help, and lest by our silence we might be guilty of that ruin and slavery which without your speedy help is like to fall upon us, yourselves and the whole nation, we have presumed to spread our cause thus plainly and largely before you; and do most earnestly entreat that you will stir up your affections to a zealous love and tender regard of the people who have chosen and trusted you, and that you will seriously consider that the end of their trust was freedom and deliverance from all kind of grievances and oppressions.

1. And that therefore in the first place, you will be exceeding careful to preserve your just authority from all prejudices of a negative voice in any person or persons whomsoever which may disable you from making that happy return unto the people which they justly expect; and that you will not be induced to lay by your strength until you have satisfied your understandings in the undoubted security of yourselves and of those who have voluntarily and faithfully adhered unto you in all your extremities and until you have secured and settled the commonwealth in solid peace and true freedom, which is the end of the primitive institution of all governments.

2. That you will take off all sentences, fines and imprisonments imposed on commoners, by any whomsoever, without due course of law or judgement of their equals, and to give due reparations to all those who have been so injuriously dealt withal; and for preventing the like for time to come, that you will enact all such arbitrary proceedings to be capital crimes.

3. That you will permit no authority whatsoever to compel any person or persons to answer to questions against themselves or nearest relations, except in cases of private interest between party and party in a legal way; and to release all such as suffer by imprisonment or otherwise for refusing to answer to such interrogatories.

4. That all statutes, oaths and covenants may be repealed so far as they tend, or may be construed, to the molestation and ensnaring of religious, peaceable, well-affected people for nonconformity or different opinion or practice in religion.

5. That no man, for preaching or publishing his opinion in religion in a peaceable way, may be punished or persecuted as heretical by judges (that are not infallible but may be mistaken as well as other men in their judgements) lest upon pretence of suppressing errors, sects or schisms, the most necessary truths and sincere professors thereof may be suppressed, as upon the like pretence it has been in all ages.

6. That you will, for the encouragement of industrious people, dissolve that old oppressive company of Merchant Adventurers and the like, and prevent all such others by great penalties, forever.

7. That you will settle a just, speedy, plain and unburdensome way for deciding of controversies and suits in law, and reduce all laws to the nearest agreement with Christianity, and publish them in the English tongue; and that all processes and proceedings therein may be true, and also in English, and in the most usual character of writing, without any abbreviations, that each one who can read may the better understand their own affairs; and that the duty of all judges, officers and practisers in the law, and of all magistrates and officers in the commonwealth, may be prescribed and their fees limited, under strict penalties, and published in print to the view and knowledge of all men: by which just and equitable means this nation shall be forever freed of an oppression more burdensome and troublesome than all the oppressions hitherto by this Parliament removed.

8. That the life of no person may be taken away but under the testimony of two witnesses at least, of honest conversation; and that in an equitable way you will proportion punishments to offences, that so no man's life may be taken, his body punished, nor his estate forfeited, but upon such weighty and considerable causes as justly deserve such punishments; and that all prisoners may have a speedy trial, that they be neither starved nor their families ruined by long and lingering imprisonment; and that imprisonment may be used only for safe custody until time of trial, and not as a punishment for offences.

9. That tithes and all other enforced maintenance may be forever abolished and nothing in place thereof imposed, but that all ministers may be paid only by those who voluntarily chose them and contract with them for their labours.

10. That you will take some speedy and effectual course to relieve all such prisoners for debt as are altogether unable to pay, that they may not perish in prison through the hard-heartedness of their creditors; and that all such as have any estates may be enforced to make payment accordingly and not shelter themselves in prison to defraud their creditors.

11. That none may be prison-keepers but such as are of approved honesty, and that they may be prohibited under great penalties to receive or detain any person or persons without lawful warrant; that their usage of prisoners may be with gentleness and civility, their fees moderate and certain, and that they may give security for the good behaviour of their under-officers.

12. That you will provide some powerful means to keep men, women and children from begging and wickedness, that this nation may be no longer a shame to Christianity therein.

13. That you will restrain and discountenance the malice and impudency of impious persons in their reviling and reproaching the well-affected with the ignominious titles of Roundheads, factious, seditious and the like, whereby your real friends have been a long time, and still are, exceedingly wronged, discouraged and made obnoxious to rude and profane people. And that you will not exclude any of approved fidelity from bearing office of trust in the commonwealth for nonconformity: rather neuters and such as manifest disaffection or opposition to common freedom, the admission and continuation of such being the chief cause of all our grievances.

These remedies, or what other shall seem more effectual to your grave wisdoms, we humbly pray may be speedily applied; and that in doing thereof you will be confident of the assistance of your petitioners and of all considerate, well-minded people to the uttermost of their best abilities, against all opposition whatsoever, looking upon ourselves as more concerned now at last to make a good end than at the first to have made a good beginning. For what shall it profit us, or what remedy can we expect, if now after so great troubles and miseries this nation should be left by this Parliament in so great a thraldom, both of body, mind and estate?

We beseech you therefore that with all your might whilst you have time, freedom and power, so effectively to fulfil the true end of Parliaments in delivering this nation from these and all other grievances, that none may presume or dare to introduce the like forever.

And we trust the God of your good success will manifest the sincerity of our intentions herein, and that our humble desires are such as tend not only to our own particular but to the general good of the commonwealth, and proper for this honourable House to grant, without which this nation cannot be safe or happy. And that He will bless you with true Christian fortitude, suitable to the trust and greatness of the work you have undertaken, and make the memory of this Parliament blessed to all succeeding generations.

Shall ever be the prayer of your humble petitioners.

3

EXTRACTS FROM 'THE HEADS OF THE PROPOSALS'

July 1647

'The heads of the proposals' were the terms for settlement offered by the army to Charles I in July 1647. They would have established a constitutional monarchy with a strong executive, and their apparent generosity to the king became a source of anxiety and fear among some in the army and London. The 'Proposals' remained a viable basis for a settlement until Charles escaped from the army's custody at Hampton Court in mid-November 1647.

The heads of the proposals agreed upon by his Excellency Sir Thomas Fairfax[1] and the Council of the Army,[2] to be tendered to the commissioners of Parliament residing with the army, and with them to be treated on by the commissioners of the army: containing the particulars of their desires in pursuance of their former declarations and papers,[3] in order to the clearing and securing of the rights and liberties of the kingdom, and the settling a just and lasting peace. To which are added some further particular desires (for the removing and redressing of divers present pressing grievances), being also comprised in or necessary pursuance of their former representations and papers appointed to be treated upon.

I. That (the things hereafter proposed, being provided for by this Parliament) a certain period may by Act of Parliament be set for the ending of this Parliament (such period to be within a year at most), and in the same Act provision to be made for the succession and constitution of Parliaments in future, as follows:

    1. That Parliaments may biennially be called and meet at a certain day, with such provision for the certainty thereof, as in the late Act was made

for triennial Parliaments; and what further or other provision shall be found needful by the Parliament to reduce it to more certainty; and upon the passing of this, the said Act for triennial Parliaments to be repealed.

2. Each biennial Parliament to sit 120 days certain, unless adjourned or dissolved sooner by their own consent; afterwards to be adjournable or dissolvable by the king; and no Parliament to sit past 240 days from their first meeting, or some other limited number of days now to be agreed on; upon the expiration whereof each Parliament to dissolve of course, if not otherwise dissolved sooner.

3. The king, upon advice of the council of state,[4] in the intervals betwixt biennial Parliaments, to call a Parliament extraordinary, provided it meet above seventy days before the next biennial day, and be dissolved at least sixty days before the same, so as the course of biennial elections may never be interrupted.

4. That this Parliament and each succeeding biennial Parliament, at or before adjournment or dissolution thereof, may appoint committees to continue during the interval for such purposes as are in any of these proposals referred to such committees.

5. That the elections of the Commons for succeeding Parliaments may be distributed to all counties, or other parts or divisions of the kingdom, according to some rule of equality or proportion, so as all counties may have a number of Parliament members allowed to their choice proportionable to the respective rates they bear in the common charges and burdens of the kingdom, according to some other rule of equality or proportion, to render the House of Commons (as near as may be) an equal representative of the whole; and in order thereunto, that a present consideration be had to take off the elections of burgesses for poor decayed or inconsiderable towns, and to give some present addition to the number of Parliament members for great counties that have now less than their due proportion, to bring all (at present), as near as may be, to such a rule of proportion as aforesaid.

6. That effectual provision be made for future freedom of elections, and certainty of due returns.

7. That the House of Commons alone have the power from time to time to set down further orders and rules for the ends expressed in the two last preceding articles, so as to reduce the elections of members for that House to more and more perfection of equality in the distribution, freedom in the election, order in the proceeding thereto, and certainty in the returns, which orders and rules (in that case) to be in laws.

8. That there be a liberty for entering dissents in the House of Commons, with provision that no member be censurable for ought said or voted in the House further than to exclusion from that trust; and that only by the judgement of the House itself.

9. That the judicial power, or power of final judgement, in the Lords and Commons (and their power of exposition and application of law, without further appeal), may be cleared; and that no officer of justice, minister of state, or other person adjudged by them, may be capable of protection or pardon from the king without their advice or consent.

10. That the right and liberty of the commons of England may be cleared and vindicated as to a due exemption from any judgement, trial or other proceeding against them by the House of Peers, without the concurring judgement of the House of Commons; as also from any other judgement, sentence or proceeding against them, other than by their equals, or according to the law of the land.

11. The same Act to provide that grand jurymen may be chosen by and for the several parts or divisions of each county respectively in some equal way (and not remain as now, at the discretion of an under-sheriff to be put on or off); and that such grand jurymen for their respective counties, may at each assize present the name of persons to be made justices of the peace from time to time, as the county has need for any to be added to the commission, and at the summer assize to present the names of three persons, out of whom the king may prick one to be sheriff for the next year.

II. For the future security of Parliaments and the militia in general, in order thereunto, that it be provided by Act of Parliament:

1. That the power of the militia by sea and land during the space of ten years next ensuing shall be ordered and disposed by the Lords and Commons assembled, and to be assembled, in the Parliament or Parliaments of England, by such persons as they shall nominate and appoint for that purpose from time to time during the said space.

2. That the said power shall not be ordered, disposed or exercised by the king's majesty that now is, or by any person or persons by any authority derived from him, during the said space, or at any time hereafter by his said majesty, without the advice and consent of the said Lords and Commons, or of such committees or council in the intervals of Parliament as they shall appoint.

3. That during the same space of ten years the said Lords and Commons may by bill or ordinance raise and dispose of what monies and for what forces they shall from time to time find necessary; as also for payment of the public debts and damages, and for all other the public uses of the kingdom.

4. And to the end the temporary security intended by the three particulars last precedent may be the better assured, it may therefore be provided: that no subjects that have been in hostility against the Parliament in the late war shall be capable of bearing any office of power or public trust in the commonwealth during the space of five years, without the consent of Parliament or of the council of state; or to sit as members or assistants of either House of Parliament, until the second biennial Parliament be passed. [. . .]

IV. That an Act be passed for disposing the great offices for ten years by the Lords and Commons in Parliament, or by such committees as they shall appoint for that purpose in the intervals (with submission to the approbation of the next Parliament), and after ten years they to nominate three, and the king out of that number to appoint one for the succession upon any vacancy. [. . .]

VI. That an Act be passed for recalling and making void all declarations and other proceedings against the Parliament, or against any that have acted by or under their authority in the late war, or in relation to it; and that the ordinances for indemnity may be confirmed.[5] [. . .]

XI. An Act to be passed to take away all coercive power, authority and jurisdiction of bishops and all other ecclesiastical officers whatsoever, extending to any civil penalties upon any; and to repeal all laws whereby the civil magistracy has been or is bound upon any ecclesiastical censure to proceed (*ex officio*[6]) unto any civil penalties against any persons so censured.

XII. That there be a repeal of all Acts or clauses in any Act enjoining the use of the Book of Common Prayer, and imposing any penalties for neglect thereof; as also of all Acts or clauses in any Act imposing any penalty for not coming to church, or for meetings elsewhere for prayer or other religious duties, exercises or ordinances; and some other provision to be made for discovering of papists and popish recusants, and for disabling of them, and of all Jesuits or priests from disturbing the state.

XIII. That the taking of the Covenant be not enforced upon any, nor any penalties imposed upon the refusers, whereby men might be restrained to take it against their judgements or consciences, but all orders and ordinances tending to that purpose to be repealed.

XIV. That (the things here before proposed being provided, for settling and securing the rights, liberties, peace and safety of the kingdom) his majesty's person, his queen, and royal issue, may be restored to a condition of safety, honour and freedom in this nation, without diminution to their personal rights, or further limitation to the exercise of the regal power than according to the particulars foregoing. [. . .]

XVI. That there may be a general Act of Oblivion to extend unto all (except the persons to be continued in exception as before[7]), to absolve from all trespasses, misdemeanours, etc. done in prosecution of the war; and from all trouble or prejudice for or concerning the same (after their compositions[8] passed), and to restore them to all privileges etc. belonging to other subjects, provided as in the fourth particular under the second general head foregoing concerning security. [. . .]

Next to the proposals aforesaid for the present settling of a peace, we shall desire that no time may be lost by the Parliament for despatch of other things tending to the welfare, ease and just satisfaction of the kingdom, and in special manner:

I. That the just and necessary liberty of the people to represent their grievances and desires by way of petition may be cleared and vindicated, according to the fifth head in the late representation or declaration of the army sent from St Albans.

II. That in pursuance of the same head in the said declaration the common grievances of the people may be speedily considered of, and effectually redressed[9] [. . .].

IV. That according to the seventh head in the said declaration an effectual course may be taken that the kingdom may be righted and satisfied in point of accounts for the vast sums that have been levied.

V. That provision may be made for payment of arrears to the army, and the rest of the soldiers of the kingdom who have concurred with the army in the late desires and proceedings thereof; and in the next place for payment of the public debts and damages of the kingdom: and that to be performed, first to such persons whose debts or damages upon the public account are great, and their estates small, so as they are thereby reduced to a difficulty of subsistence – in order to all which, and to the fourth particular last proceeding, we shall speedily offer some further particulars

4

EXTRACTS FROM 'THE CASE OF THE ARMY TRULY STATED'

October 1647

Presented to Fairfax on 18 October 1647, 'The case of the army truly stated'
articulated the genuine apprehension that 'The heads of the proposals' induced
among some of the army. The pamphlet is disorganised and an obvious composite
work, though whether the agents[1] who put their names to it were its sole authors
remains open to question. Other soldiers may well have contributed, perhaps even
some civilians.

The case of the army truly stated, together with the mischiefs and dangers
that are imminent, and some suitable remedies. Humbly proposed by the
agents of five regiments of horse to their respective regiments and the
whole army, as it was presented [. . .] October 18 1647 unto his
Excellency Sir Thomas Fairfax. [. . .] Deuteronomy 20:8: What man
is there that is fearful and faint hearted? Let him go and return unto his
house, least his brethren's heart faint as well as his heart.
Judges 7:7: And the Lord said unto Gideon, by the three hundred men
that lapped will I save you, and deliver the Midianites into thine hand:
and let all the other people go, every man unto his place.
London. Printed in the year 1647.

Whereas the grievances, dissatisfactions and desires of the army, both as
commoners and soldiers, has been many months since represented to the
Parliament, and the army has waited with much patience to see their
common grievances redressed and the rights and freedoms of the nation
cleared and secured; yet upon a most serious and conscientious view of
our narratives, representations, engagement, declarations, remonstrances,

and comparing with those the present state of the army and kingdom, and the present manner of actings of many at the headquarters, we not only apprehend nothing to have been done effectually, either for the army or the poor oppressed people of the nation, but we also conceive that there is little probability of any good without some more speedy and vigorous actings.

In respect of the army there has been hitherto no public vindication thereof about their first petition,[2] answerable to the ignominy of declaring them enemies to the state and disturbers of the peace; no public clearing nor repairing of the credit of the officers sent for about that petition as delinquents; no provision for apprentices, widows, orphans or maimed soldiers, answerable to our reasonable addresses propounded in their behalf; no such indemnity as provides security for the quiet, ease or safety of the soldiers disbanded or to be disbanded; no security for our arrears, or provision for present pay to enable the army to subsist without burdening the distressed country.

And in respect to the rights and freedoms of ourselves and the people that we declared we would insist upon, we conceive there is no kind or degree of satisfaction given. There is no determinate period of time set when the Parliament shall certainly end. The House is in no measure purged, either from persons unduly elected or from delinquents that appeared to be such at the army's last insisting upon their rights, or since; the honour of the Parliamentary authority not cleared and vindicated from the most horrid injustice of that declaration against the army for petitioning, nor of suppressing and burning petitions, abusing and imprisoning petitioners: but those strange precedents remain upon record to the infamy of Parliamentary authority and the danger of our own and the people's freedoms. The people are not righted nor satisfied in point of accounts for the vast sums of money disbursed by them. None of the public burdens or oppressions by arbitrary committees, injustice in the law, tithes, monopolies and restraint of free trade, burdensome oaths, inequality of assessments, excise and otherwise are removed or lightened. The rights of the people in their Parliaments concerning the nature and extent of that power are not cleared and declared. So that we apprehend our own and the people's case little (if in any measure) better since the army last hazarded themselves for their own and the people's rights and freedoms.

No, to the grief of our hearts we must declare that we conceive the people and the army's case much impaired since the first rendezvous at

Newmarket when that solemn engagement was entered into, and that from the consideration that the army's engagement, representations, declarations and remonstrances (and promises in them contained) are declined, and more and more daily broken; and not only in some smaller matters wherein the army and the kingdom are not so nearly concerned, but in divers particulars of dangerous consequence to the army and the whole nation. As:

First, in the engagement, page 5, the army promised – every member thereof, each to other and to the Parliament and kingdom – that they would neither disband nor divide, nor suffer themselves to be disbanded or divided, until satisfaction should be given to the army in relation to their grievances and desires, and security that neither the army nor the freeborn people of England should remain subject to such injuries, oppression and abuse, as the corrupt party in the Parliament then had attempted against them.

Secondly, the train of artillery is now to be disbanded before satisfaction or security is given to the whole army in relation to themselves or other the freeborn people, either in respect to their grievances or desires. And when the strength or sinews of the army be broken, what effectual good can be secured for themselves or the people in case of opposition?

Thirdly, the army is divided into quarters so far distant that one part is in no capability to give timely assistance to another if any design should be to disband any part by violence suddenly, although neither our grievances nor desires as soldiers or commoners are redressed or answered. And as we conceive this dividing of the army before satisfaction or security (as aforesaid) to be contrary to the army's intention in their engagement at the said rendezvous, so we conceive it has from that time given all the advantage to the enemies to band and design against the army, whereby not only pay has been kept from the soldiers, and security for arrears prevented, but the kingdom was endangered to have been embroiled in blood, and the settlement of the peace and freedom of the nation has been thus long delayed.

The whole intent of the engagement and the equitable sense of it has been perverted openly by affirming, and by sinister means making seeming determinations in the council,[3] that the army was not to insist upon or demand any security for any of their own or other the freeborn people's freedoms or rights, though they might propound anything to the Parliament's consideration. And according to that high breach of their engagement, their actions have been regulated, and nothing that was declared formerly to be insisted upon has been resolvedly adhered to, or claimed as the army's or the people's due. And we conceive it has been by this means that the soldier has had no pay constantly provided, nor any security for arrears given them, and that hitherto they could not obtain so much as to be paid-up equally with those that did desert the army [. . .].

Fourthly, in the prosecution of this breach there has been many discouragements of the agitators[4] of the regiments in consulting about the most effectual means for procuring the speedy redress of the people's grievances, and clearing and securing the native rights of the army and all others the free commons. It has been instilled into them that they ought not to intermeddle with those matters, thereby to induce them to betray the trust the regiments reposed in them; and for that purpose the endeavours of some has been to persuade the soldiery that their agitators have meddled with more than concerned them. [. . .]

Sixthly, in the declaration of June 14, page 6, it is declared that the army took up arms in judgement and conscience for the people's just rights and liberties, and not as mercenary soldiers, hired to serve an arbitrary power of the state; and that in the same manner it continued in arms at that time, and page 7 of the same declaration, it was declared that they proceeded upon the principles of right and freedom, and upon the law of nature and nations. But the strength of the endeavours of many has been and are now spent to persuade the soldiers and agitators that they stand as soldiers only to serve the state, and may not as free commons claim their right and freedom as due to them, as those ends for which they have hazarded their lives, and that the ground of their refusing to disband was only the want of arrears and indemnity. [. . .]

Eighthly, in the declaration of June 14, page 10 (as in all other remonstrances and declarations), it was desired that the rights and liberties of the people might be secured before the king's business should be considered. But now the grievances of the people are propounded to be considered after the restoring him to the regal power, and that in such a way according to the 'Proposals', viz., with a negative voice, that the people that have purchased by blood what was their right, of which the king endeavoured to deprive them, should yet solely depend on his will for their relief in their grievances and oppressions. And in like manner the security for the army's arrears is proposed to be considered after the business of the king be determined, so that there is a total declension since the method formerly desired in the settling of the peace of the nation.

Ninthly, it has been always professed and declared that the army was called forth and conjured by the Parliament's declarations for defence of the people's rights against the forces raised by the king, and for delivering the king from his evil council, who seduced him to raise the war, and bringing delinquents to condign punishment. But now through the army's countenance and indulgence, those conquered enemies that were the king's forces abuse, reproach and again insult over the people, whose freedom was the grounds of the army's engagement. Indeed, the king's evil counsellors that concurred in designing all the mischiefs in the king's late war against the people, are again restored to him, and are admitted free access without check into all the army's quarrels, whereby they are restored to a capacity of plotting and designing mischief against the army and kingdom. [. . .]

Thus all promises of the army to the people that petitioned his Excellency and the army to stand for the national interest, freedoms and rights, are hitherto wholly declined, and the law of nature and nations now refused by many to be the rule by which their proceedings should be regulated. They now strip themselves of the interest of Englishmen, which was so ill-resented when it was attempted by the malice of the enemies. And thus the people's expectations that were much greatened, and their hopes of relief in their miseries and oppressions which were so much heightened, are like to be frustrate. And while you look for peace and freedom, the flood-gates of slavery, oppression and misery are opened upon the nation, as may appear by the present manifold dangers that encompass about the army and the whole nation.

The mischiefs, evils and dangers which are and will be the necessary consequence of the army's declining or delaying the effectual fulfilling of its first engagement, promises and declarations, or of its neglect to insist positively upon its first principles of common right and freedom. [. . .]

First, the love and affection of the people to the army (which is an army's greatest strength) is decayed, cooled and near lost. It's already the common voice of the people, 'What good have our new saviours done for us? What grievances have they procured to be redressed? Wherein is our condition bettered?', or 'How are we more free than before?'.

Secondly, not only so, but the army is rendered as an heavy burden to the people, in regard more pay is exacted daily for them, and the people find no good procured by them that's answerable or equivalent to the charge. So that now the people begin to cry louder for disbanding the army than they did formerly for keeping us in arms because they see no benefit accruing. They say they are as likely to be oppressed and enslaved both by king and Parliament as they were before the army engaged professedly to see their freedoms cleared and secured. [. . .]

Sixthly, through the same declension of the army's first principles – and the good and necessary method propounded for settling the nation in peace and freedom before the king's business be considered – the king is likely to recover his old capacity before the people's freedoms (which they have redeemed out of the hands of him and his forces by blood) be cleared and established securely, and likewise before any security be given for arrears. And then what probability there is that then there should be any good security of pay obtained for the army that conquered him, and for the freedoms of those that assisted them, let any rational man judge? It may more certainly be expected that he will provide for the pay and arrears of his own soldiery rather than of ours. And likewise by the same means, the army's and their assistants' indemnity is propounded to receive its strength from the king's consent: whereas not only his signing of, or consent to any act, is wholly null and void in law because he is under restraint, and so our indemnity will be insufficient if it shall depend in the least on his confirmation; but also it's the highest disparagement to the supreme authority of this nation – the Parliament – that when they have commanded an army upon service against the king, they should not have sufficient power to save them harmless for obedience to their commands. And also it's the highest dishonour to the army that they should seek to the conquered enemy to save them harmless for fighting against them, which is to ask him pardon, and so will remain as a perpetual reproach upon them. [. . .]

Now we cannot but declare that these sad apprehensions of mischiefs, dangers and confusion gaping to devour the army have filled our hearts with troubles, that we never did, nor do regard the worst of evils or mischiefs that can befall ourselves in comparison to the consequence of them to the poor nation, or to the security of common right and freedom. We could not but, in real (not formal, feigned) trouble of heart for the poor nation and oppressed people, break forth and cry, 'O our bowels! Our bowels! We are troubled at the very heart to hear the people's doleful groans.' And yet their expected deliverers will not hear or consider. They have run to and fro, and sighed or even wept forth their sorrows and miseries in petitions, first to the king, then to the Parliament, and then to the army; yet they have all been like broken reeds: even the army itself (upon whom they leaned) have pierced their hands. Their eyes even fail with looking for peace and freedom, but behold nothing but distraction, oppression and trouble; and could we hope that help is intended, yet the people perish by delays. We wish therefore that the bowels of compassion in the whole army might yearn towards their distressed brethren, and that they might with one consent say each to other, 'Come let us join together speedily to demand present redress for the people's grievances and security for all their and our own rights and freedoms as soldiers and commoners. Let us never divide each from other till those just demands be answered really and effectually, that so for the people's ease as many forces as are not absolutely necessary may be speedily disbanded and our honour may be preserved unspotted, when they shall see that we minded not our own interest, but the good, freedom and welfare of the whole Nation.' Now to all that shall thus appear we propound:

1. That whatsoever was proposed to be insisted on either in the declaration of June the 14, or the remonstrance of June 23 and in the remonstrance from Kingston, August 18, be adhered to resolvedly, so as not to recede from those desires until they be thoroughly and effectually answered. More particularly, that whereas it appears by positive laws and ancient just customs that the people have right to new, successive elections for Parliaments at certain periods of time, and that it ought not to be denied them, being so essential to their freedom that without it they are no better than slaves (the nature of that legislative power being arbitrary). And that therefore it be insisted on so positively and resolvedly, as not to recede from it.

2. That a determined period of time be forthwith set wherein this Parliament shall certainly be dissolved, provided also that the said period be within 9 or 10 months next ensuing, that so there may be sufficient time for settling of peace and freedom.

3. Whereas all good is obstructed and diverted by the power and influence of delinquents, the late usurpers and undue elected ones in the Parliament, that therefore it be positively and resolvedly insisted on, that the house be forthwith purged from all that have forfeited their trust, or were unduly elected [. . .].

5. Whereas Parliaments rightly constituted are the foundation of hopes of right and freedom to this people, and whereas the people have been

prevented of Parliaments, though many positive laws have been made for a constant succession of Parliaments; that therefore it be positively and resolvedly insisted upon that a law paramount be made, enacting it to be unalterable by Parliaments, that the people shall of course meet without any warrants or writs once in every two years upon an appointed day in their respective counties, for the election of the representers in Parliament; and that all the freeborn at the age of 21 years and upwards be the electors, excepting those that have or shall deprive themselves of that their freedom, either for some years, or wholly by delinquency; and that the Parliament so elected and called may have a certain period of time set, wherein they shall of course determine, and that before the same period they may not be adjournable and dissolvable by the king, or any other except themselves.

6. Whereas all power is originally and essentially in the whole body of the people of this nation, and whereas their free choice or consent by their representers is the only original or foundation of all just government, and the reason and end of the choice of all just governors whatsoever is their apprehension of safety and good by them; that it be insisted upon positively, that the supreme power of the people's representers, or Commons assembled in Parliament, be forthwith clearly declared as: their power to make laws, or repeal laws (which are not, or ought not to be unalterable); as also their power to call to an account all officers in this nation whatsoever, for their neglect or treacheries in their trust for the people's good, and to continue or displace and remove them from their offices, dignities or trust, according to their demerits by their faithfulness or treachery in the business or matters where with they are entrusted; and further, that this power to constitute any kind of governors or officers that they shall judge to be for the people's good be declared, and that, upon the aforesaid considerations, it be insisted upon, that all obstructions to the freedom and equality of the people's choice of their representers, either by patents, charters or usurpations by pretended customs, be removed by these present Commons in Parliament, and that such a freedom of choice be provided for, as the people may be equally represented. This power of Commons in Parliament is the thing against which the king has contended, and the people have defended with their lives, and therefore ought now to be demanded as the price of their blood.

7. That all the oppressions of the poor by excise upon beer, cloth stuffs, and all manufactories and English commodities, be forthwith taken

off, and that all excise be better regulated, and imposed upon foreign commodities, and a time set wherein it shall certainly end, if there be a necessity of its present continuance on such commodities. [. . .]

And it is further offered, in consideration that the court have occasioned the late war, and reduced the state to such necessity by causing such vast expense of treasure, that therefore whereas the many oppressions of the people, and the danger of absolute tyranny, were the occasion of the expense of so much blood, and whereas the people have bought their rights and freedoms by the price of blood, and have in vain waited long since the common enemy has been subdued for the redress of their grievances and oppressions; that therefore it be demanded as the people's due, which ought not to be denied to the army or to them yet seeing the king has his court and lives in honour, yet before his business be further considered, because the people are under much oppression and misery, it be forthwith the whole work of the Parliament to hear, consider of, and study effectually redress for, all common grievances and oppressions, and for the securing all other the people's rights and freedoms, besides all these aforementioned, and in particular:

That all the orders, votes, ordinances or declarations, that have passed either to discountenance petitions, suppress, prevent or burn petitions, imprison or declare against petitioners – being dangerous precedents against the freedom of the people – may be forthwith expunged out of the journal books, and the injustice of them clearly declared to all the people; and that in such a declaration the soldiery be vindicated as to the right and equity of their first petition. [. . .]

And it's further offered, that whereas millions of money have been kept in dead stocks in the City of London, the halls and companies, and the freemen of the city could never obtain any account thereof according to their right, that therefore a just and strict account may be forthwith given to all the freemen of all those dead stocks; and yet whereas there has been nothing paid out of those, nor for the lands pertaining to the city, while the estates of others have been much wasted by continual payments, that therefore proportionable sums to what other estates have paid may be taken out of those dead stocks and lands, which would amount to such vast sums as would pay much of the soldiers' arrears without burdening the oppressed people.

And it's further offered, that forest lands, and deans' and chapters' lands be immediately set apart for the arrears of the army, and that the revenue of these, and the residue of bishops' lands unsold, till the time of sale may be forthwith appointed to be paid unto our treasury, to be reserved for the soldiers' constant pay. And it's to be wished that only such part of the aforesaid lands be sold as necessity requires to satisfy the soldiery for arrears, and that the residue be reserved and improved for a constant revenue for the state, that the people may not be burdened, and that out of the revenues public debts may be paid and not first taken out of their own purses to be repaid to them. [. . .]

And whereas it's conceived that the fees of receivers of customs and excise, if they were justly computed, would amount to near as much as the army's pay, it's therefore offered that speedy consideration be had of the multitude of those officers and their excessive fees and profits [. . .].

And for the ease and satisfaction of the people it's further to be insisted on that the charge of all the forces to be kept up in the kingdom by sea or land be particularly computed and published, and that all taxes that shall be necessary may be wholly proportioned, according to that charge; and that there be an equal rate propounded throughout the kingdom in all assessments [. . .].[5]

That it be insisted on that such indemnity be forthwith given both for the soldiery and all that gave them assistance, and shall provide securely for their quiet, ease and safety, and prevent all chargeable journeys to London to seek after and wait upon committees. [. . .]

Whereas mercy and justice are the foundations of a lasting peace, it's necessary to be insisted on (for the healing differences as far as possible) that all those whose estates have been sequestered and yet were not in arms for the king (or gave any actual assistance to him in men, money or arms, plate, horse, etc. in the late war), that all such be discharged forthwith from their sequestrations; and that all such as have compounded may not be enforced to pay the five or twentieth part, seeing their whole estates were so long under sequestration. And that all those that have not compounded who were in arms for the king may be compelled forthwith to compound, provided that their compositions be so moderate as none may exceed two years' revenue, that their families be not ruined, and they put upon desperate attempts against the peace of the nation to preserve themselves.

These things propounded are no more than what we conceived should have been thoroughly done long since, being as to the principle of them but the substance and equitable sense of our former declarations, remonstrances and representations. And therefore though our restless desires of the people's good and of the welfare of the army have constrained us thus publicly to state our case and the remedy, according to the best improvement of the small talent of understanding that God has given freely to us, yet let not the matter be prejudged because of the unworthy authors; neither let it be thought presumption. It may be remembered that the father's danger made a dumb child to speak, and the army's, indeed all the people's dangers and miseries have wrested open our mouths, who had otherwise been silent in this kind to the grave.

And let it not be thought that we intend the division of the army; we profess we are deeply sensible and desire all our fellow soldiers to consider it. In case the union of the army should be broken (which the enemy wait for), ruin and destruction will break in upon us like a roaring sea. But we are much confident that the adhering to those desires and to that speedy way of attaining our just ends for which we first engaged, cannot be interpreted to be a desire of division, but the strongest vigorous endeavours after union. And though many whom we did betrust have been guilty of most supine negligence, yet we expect that the same instruction of judgement and conscience that we have all professed did command us forth at first for the people's freedom, will be again so effectual that all will unanimously concur with us, so that a demand of the people's and army's rights shall be made by the whole army as by one man, that then all the enemies to, or obstructers of the happy settlement of common right, peace and freedom, may hear of our union and resolution, and their hands may be weak, and their hearts may fail them. And so this army that God has clothed with honour in subduing the common enemy, may yet be more honourable in the people's eyes, when they shall be called the repairers of their breaches, and the restorers of their peace, right and freedom.

And this is the prayer, and shall always be the earnest endeavours of the army's and all the people's most faithful servants,

Lieutenant-General's } regiment	Robert Everard[6] George Sadler	Commissary-General's } regiment	George Garret Thomas Beverley
Colonel Fleetwood's } regiment	William Prior William Bryan	Colonel Whalley's regiment	Matthew Weale William Russell Richard Seale
Colonel Rich's regiment	John Dover William Hudson Agitators		

Guildford, October 9 1647.

[. . .] Upon the presentation to and serious perusal thereof by his Excellency, the sum of his answer was to this effect. That he judged their intentions were honest, and desired that everyone of a public spirit would be acting for the public, and that for his part he had freely ventured his life for common right and freedom and should freely engage it again, adding further that he thought it meet it should be presented to the General Council.

5

EXTRACTS FROM 'A CALL TO ALL THE SOLDIERS OF THE ARMY'

October 1647

Although the agents claimed that 'The case of the army' was warmly received by Fairfax, it was denounced by other army commanders. This provoked an incendiary response in the anonymous 'A call to all the soldiers of the army', which contained an open incitement to mutiny. Published around the time of the beginning of the Putney debates, the pamphlet is thought to be the work of John Wildman,[1] a civilian ally of the agents.

A call to all the soldiers of the army by the free people of England. 1. Justifying the proceedings of the five regiments. 2. Manifesting the necessity of the whole army's joining with them in all their faithful endeavours, both for removing of all tyranny and oppression [. . .], and establishing the just liberties and peace of this nation. 3. Discovering (without any respect of persons) the chief authors, contrivers and increasers of all our miseries, especially the new raised hypocrites, by whose treacherous practices all the just intentions and actions of the agitators and other well-minded soldiers have been made fruitless.

Isaiah 58:6: Is not this the fast that I have chosen? To loose the bands of wickedness, to undo the heavy burdens, and to let the oppressed go free, and that to break every yoke?

Matthew 23:27-8: Woe unto you scribes and Pharisees, hypocrites; for you are like unto whited sepulchres, which indeed appear beautiful outward, but are within full of dead men's bones and all uncleanness.

Even so you also outwardly appear righteous unto men, but within you are full of hypocrisy and iniquity.
Printed in the year 1647.

To those five regiments of the army who have already declared themselves to stand for maintenance of our just liberties, and for removal of those heavy oppressions mentioned in that worthy discourse entitled 'The case of the army'; and to all who intend to join timely and speedily with them.

You true lovers of justice and the commonwealth, the work which you have undertaken is so just and necessary that you cannot but be exceedingly comforted in the very thoughts thereof. You have justice and necessity on your side, which will powerfully draw all free-principled men of all estates and conditions unto you; nor can you fail of good success unless contrary to the will and mind of God, who has moved your hearts and raised you to this excellent, eminent and needful a work, you give ear in anyway to the siren-songs of flatterers, temporisers, neuters and hypocrites. [. . .]

Take heed of crafty politicians and subtle machiavellians, and be sure to trust no man's painted words; it being high time now to see actions, yes, and those constantly upright too. If any man (by bringing forth unexpected bitter fruits) has drawn upon himself a just suspicion, let him justly bear his own blame; such a one is no more to be trusted whatsoever be pretended until he as far exceed others, as he has come short, in prosecution of your just ends and purposes.

One of the surest marks of deceivers is to make fair, long and eloquent speeches, but a trusty or true-hearted man studies more to do good actions than utter deceitful orations. And one of the surest tokens of confederates in evil is not only, when one of his fellows is vehement, fiery or hot in any of their pursuits, to be patient, cold or moderate, to pacify his partner, and like deceitful lawyers before their clients to qualify matters, but sometimes seem to discord or fall out, and quarrel in counsels, reasonings and debates, and yet nevertheless in the end to agree in evil; which they do purposely to hold upright men in a charitable (though doubtful) opinion, that if such and such a man be not godly and upright, they know not whom in the world to trust, while in the mean time under the vizards[2] of great professions, gilded with some religious actions, they both deceive the world and bring their wicked designs and self-interests to pass.

Those of you that use your Thursday General Councils of late might have observed so much of this kind of juggling, falsehood and double-dealing, as might have served to some good use at this point of extremity. But truly most that have been there have been deluded, to our great grief, which appears by the unreasonable proceedings of that court, as in many things, so especially in their debates about the aforesaid 'Case of the army', now published and subscribed by you. Wherein though the general was so ingenuous as to move for the public reading thereof, yet the Commissary-General Ireton[3] and Lieutenant-General Cromwell,[4] yes, and most of the court, would and did proceed to censure and judge both it and the authors and promoters thereof, without reading it, and ever since do impudently boast and glory in that their victory. [. . .]

In the council they held forth to you the bloody flag of threats and terrors, talked of nothing but faction, dividing principles, anarchy, of hanging, punishing, yes, and impudently maintained that your regiments were abused and the aforesaid 'Case' not truly subscribed, and did appoint a committee *ad terrorem*.[5] And abroad[6] they hold forth the white flag of accommodation and satisfaction, and of minding the same thing which you mind, and to be flesh of your flesh and bone of your bone, and to invite you to their headquarters, where they hope either to work upon you as they have most lamentably done upon others, even to betray your trust, confound both your understandings and counsels, corrupt your judgements, and blast your actions. And though they should not prevail with you, yet there they keep so great a state and distance that they suppose you will not dare to make good the things you have published.

But if you be as wise as you had need, keep both from thence altogether, and as much at a distance from these pretended friends as you did once from open enemies. Believe it, if you please, you may as well hazard at Hampton Court as where they are, for the king and they become one, as by the ensuing discourse is made manifest.

If you do adventure to go thither, beware that you be not frightened by the word 'anarchy', unto a love of monarchy, which is but the gilded name for tyranny; for anarchy had never been so much as once mentioned amongst you had it not been for that wicked end. 'Tis an old threadbare trick of the profane court and does amongst discreet men show plainly who is for the court and against the liberties of the people, who, when so ever they positively insist for their just freedoms, are immediately flapped in the mouths with these most malignant reproaches: 'Oh, you are for anarchy; you are against all government; you are sectaries, seditious persons, troublers both of church and state, and so not worthy to live in a commonwealth. There shall be a speedy course taken both against you and such as you. Away with all such from Parliament-doors and Headquarters!' And if you can escape these delusions (as through God's assistance, we trust, you will), and not be satisfied with half or quarter remedies, or things holding a shadow only of good without the substance, we cannot in the least doubt of your good success, being firmly resolved to stand by you and to live and die with you.

You had need to be well armed and fortified against the devices that will be put upon you. Ireton, you know, has already scandalized 'The case of the army' in the General Council, where, by his own and his confederate's craft and policy, he reigns as sole master, in so much as those friends you have there (which we hope you will see in due time not to be few) find it to little purpose to show themselves active in opposing him. And as he undertook so has he answered your 'Case'; wherein he shows himself so full of art and cunning, smooth delusion (being skilled in nothing more), that if you did not sensibly know the things to be really and experimentally true, which you have therein expressed and published, 'tis ten to one but he would deceive you.

This is certain: in the House of Commons both he and his father Cromwell do so earnestly and palpably carry on the king's design that your best friends there are amazed thereat, and even ready to weep for grief to see such a sudden and dangerous alteration. And this they do in the name of the whole army, certifying the House that if they do not make further address to the king, they cannot promise that the army will stand by them if they should find opposition. And what is this but as much in effect as in the name of the whole army to threaten the House into a compliance with the king, your most deadly enemy, and who, if things go on thus, will deceive both you and them, yes, and all that act most for him?

To what purpose then should you either debate, confer or treat with such false sophisters or treacherous deceivers as these, who, like the former courtiers, can always play the hypocrites without any check of conscience? To what end should you read or spend time to consider what they either write or speak, it being so evident that as they did intend so they proceed to hold you in hand till their work be done?

But if you will show yourselves wise, stop your ears against them: resist the devil and he will fly from you. Hold not parley with them, but proceed with that just work you have so happily begun, without anymore regarding one word they speak. For their consciences being at liberty to say or do anything which may advance their own ends, they have great advantage against you whose consciences will not permit you to say or do anything but what is just and true and what you mean to perform, they having shamefully proved themselves to be large promisers, thereby to deceive both you and all the people, but the worst performers that ever lived.

And therefore, certainly, you have no warrant from God to treat either with them or their deceitful instruments, who will be speedily in great numbers sent amongst you. But as you know most of them for evil, so are you to avoid them as the most venomous serpents. And fail not in this your just enterprise to cast yourselves chiefly upon God in the use of all the knowledge, experience, means and power, wherewith he has furnished you; and secondly upon the people, who will be ready with all their might and strength to assist you whilst you are faithful and real for them. Join and be one with them in heart and hand, with all possible speed, in some substantial and firm agreement for just freedom and common right, that this nation may no longer float upon such wavering, uncertain and sandy foundations of government, which have been one of the greatest causes both of all your and our predecessors' miseries.

Otherwise, if you be not at a firm established certainty of all particulars therein conducing both to the prosperity and safety of the people, we see no other remedy but that now after all your victories, both you and we will come to live that dying life, even at the cruel mercies of most wicked tyrants and blood oppressors.

Thus you may assure yourselves, if you now suffer your strength either to be wrung or flattered out of your hands (though it be a most sad thing to speak) before many months pass, both you and we are like to be driven, yes, and even glad to beg our bread. And why is it they keep you still so poor as they have a long time done, to the great grief of us all, but that you might not be able to help or stir more than as many prisoners? Yes, they intend when they are advanced to the height of their preferment, that many, both of you and us, shall be whipped or banished as vagabonds, starved in prisons, or hanged on gallows by dozens, scores and hundreds, as thieves and murderers.

Therefore, let the foresight and consideration of these sad rewards of all our good services, which are fast hatching for us, make you wise and provident in time who have sufficient power with our assistance to defend both yourselves and us; and the rather use all lawful means to prevent, than to be in any ways forced to repent. Work whilst it is called today; the night comes on a pace, even the blackness of darkness, of a most wicked accommodation, and then no man can work. Up therefore and be doing what is just, and the Lord our God will assist you, and we shall spend our lives and estates with you. Farewell.

A call to all the soldiers of the army by the free people of England. [. . .] Until the wickedness of the House of Commons came to such a mass that they had plotted your disbanding, and thereby gave you just cause to stand upon your own guard, there appeared no hope but that we and you with all who had always stood for common freedom against both kingly, lordly and Parliamentary tyranny, should have been made the objects of their scorn and subjects of their malice, and had before this been delivered up as slaves into the cruel hands of the king their master.

But God has put it into your hearts to take care both of yourselves and us, and by your wisdom and resolution wrought a mighty alteration. You of the plainer sort were thought by him who is only wise to be the meetest[7] instruments for so great a work, and we are grieved that those who were raised by your valour to places of honour and greatness, should so soon despise the way of the Lord, and should not still make use of you in finishing the work so happily begun.

Your agitators, we hear, are esteemed but as a burden to the chief officers, which we judge to be the reason that all things now are in such a languishing condition. Our hopes die daily within us, and we fear you will too soon give yourselves and us, with our joint and just cause, into their hands. You should have considered that they a long time staggered before they engaged with you, and certainly had never engaged but that they saw no other way nor means to shelter and preserve themselves from the power of Holles and Stapleton,[8] with their confederates.

We have now too much cause to fear that your and our good, or the promoting of the common freedom of the nation was the least part of their care or intention; for they no sooner by your unanimous resolutions became masters of the king, Parliament and city, and thereby of a power to do whatever good was desirable either by you or us, but they wholly despise and neglect you. [. . .]

No just nor equal way is ordered for due and timely payment of you in the army, but is omitted of set-purpose that free quarter[9] may make you odious and incense the people against you. And nothing is now so much minded by your officers and their Parliament than how to please, satisfy and establish the king, who hates both you and us with an inveterate hatred. And were your officers of the same mind they have sometimes been, he would hate them in the like manner. But it appears he, by his insinuations, has so wrought upon their affections that he and they seem to be of one heart, and of one mind, so that all their care is to please him; and that they may do it the more effectually (swallowing up their duty to God, their engagement with you, their declaration and protestation, with all the innocent blood that he has spilt), they for his sake forbear to clear the House of so many of his trusty friends, who in the counterfeit Parliament so vehemently endeavoured his speedy coming to London, where certainly your officers earnestly desire to him: otherwise, why are they so importunate (after his denial of the propositions) to present their weak and lame 'Proposals' to the House, and so to prepare them, or some result thereof, to be sent to him for his agreement and consent? Why make they an idol of him, and bear him up so high in the eyes and fancies of the people as if he were in their esteem, the very light of their eyes and the breath of their nostrils?

Why are they so familiar with Ashburnham[10] and other his chief agents? Why permit they so many of his deceitful clergy to continue about him? Why do themselves kneel and kiss and fawn him? Why have they received favours from him, and sent their wives or daughters to visit him, or to kiss his hand, or be kissed of him?

Oh shame of men! Oh sin against God! What, to do thus to a man of blood; over head and ears in the blood of your dearest friends and fellow commoners? To him that thirsts for your blood, yes, and theirs too, however they flatter and fool themselves. Hear oh heavens, and regard oh earth, if this in these exceed not the wickedness of the most wicked upon earth?

And think you, oh friends, to escape the severe judgement of Almighty God, who by your silence and want of reproof of these things, give countenance thereunto. For your officers do not go on in these unworthy courses but that they presume upon you to back them. For alas, what are they without you, but as so many single persons ready to be hunted by all the great parties in the land? So that you are, in effect, the abettors of all their evil courses, the bawds and panderers to their adulterate practices with the king. Nor can you make amends for your so sinful neglect but by a speedy impeachment of him, and exemplary punishment of them for their private tampering with him who, if he were a politick tyrant when this Parliament began, how bloody a one has he proved himself ever since?

We beseech you therefore, yes, we beg of you all, commanders and soldiers, that are yet untainted in your integrity and have not yet bowed your knees to Baal, that you will not betray yourselves, your just cause and us, so unworthily, nor seem to distrust that power and wisdom of God by which you have done so great and mighty works, but that now you will be bold and courageous for your God and for his people, and for justice against all ungodliness and unrighteousness of men without respect of persons.

And before it be too late, deal plainly with Ireton, by whose cowardly or ambitious policy Cromwell is betrayed into these mischievous practices, and by whose craft the power of your agitators is brought to nothing, and by whose dissimulation many of them are corrupted and become treacherous unto you. None but flatterers, tale-bearers and turncoats are countenanced by him. Let him know you know him and hate his courses. Your General Councils, by his imperious carriage, are like unto Star Chambers; a plain man is made an offender for a word.

And if Cromwell instantly repent not and alter his course, let him know also that you loved and honoured just, honest, sincere and valiant Cromwell that loved his country and the liberties of the people above his life, yes, and hated the king as a man of blood, but that Cromwell ceasing to be such, he ceases to be the object of your love.

And since there is no remedy, you must begin your work anew. You are as you were at Bury.[11] You are no strangers to the way; you have already made a good beginning, wherein we rejoice. You have men amongst you as fit to govern as others to be removed. And with a word you can create new officers. Necessity has no law, and against it there is no plea. The safety of the people is above all law. And if you be not very speedy, effectual, and do your work thoroughly, and not by halves as it has been, you and we perish inevitably.

What your general is you best know, but 'tis too late to live by hopes or to run any more hazards. None can deceive you but whom you trust upon doubtful terms. Beware of the flattery and sophistry of men: bargain with your officers not to court it in fine or gaudy apparel, nor to regard titles, fine fare or compliments. Those that do are much more liable to temptations than other men. A good conscience is a continual feast, and let your outside testify that you delight not to be soldiers longer than necessity requires.

Draw yourselves into an exact council, and get amongst you the most judicious and truest lovers of the people you can find to help you, and let your end be justice without respect of persons, and peace and freedom to all sorts of peaceable people. Establish a free Parliament by expulsion of the usurpers. Free the people from all burdens and oppressions, speedily and without delay. Take an exact account of the public treasure, that public charges may be defrayed by subsidies, tithes abolished, the laws, and proceedings therein, regulated, and free-quarter abandoned.

Let nothing deter you from this, so just and necessary a work. None will oppose you therein, or so long as you continue sincere and uncorrupted. For all sorts of people have been abused: kings have abused them, Parliaments have abused them, and your chief officers have most grossly deceived the honest party. Be confident none will oppose, and be as confident that thousands and ten thousands are ready and ripe to assist you.

Be strong therefore, our dear true-hearted brethren and fellow Commoners, and be of good courage, and the Lord our God will direct you by his wisdom, who never yet failed you in your greatest extremities. Stay for no farther, look for no other call: for the voice of necessity is the call of God. All other ways for your indemnity are but delusive; and if you trust to any other under the fairest promises, you will find yourselves in a snare.

Whom can you trust, who has not hitherto deceived you? Trust only to justice: for God is a God of justice, and those that promote the same shall be preserved. Free the Parliament from those incendiaries with all your might. The true and just patriots (yes, all but deceivers) therein, long for your assistance, and, that being effectually done, you may safely put yourselves and the whole nation upon them both for provision, indemnity and just liberty. [. . .]

But in these and all other things, the wisdom and goodness of God, we trust, will be your guide to lead you into all the paths of righteousness, unto whose will and mind if you carefully give care, you shall certainly be blessed in all your undertakings.

FINIS.

6

AN AGREEMENT OF THE PEOPLE

October 1647

In spite of the opposition of some of the officers, the General Council invited the agents and their associates to join them in debate. This opportunity inspired a meeting of agents, soldiers and civilians to devise the 'Agreement of the people' – a written constitution that would gain legitimacy through a literal agreement of all the population. The dominant hand behind this revolutionary concept may well have been that of Wildman.

An agreement of the people for a firm and present peace upon grounds of common right and freedom, as it was proposed by the agents of the five regiments of horse, and since by the general approbation of the army[1] offered to the joint concurrence of all the free commons of England.

The names of the regiments which have already appeared for the case of 'The case of the army truly stated', and for this present 'Agreement', viz.

1. General's regiment	}	
2. Life-guard	}	1. General's regiment }
3. Lieutenant-General's regiment	}	2. Colonel Sir Hardress Waller's regiment }
4. Commissary-General's regiment	}	3. Colonel Lambert's regiment }
5. Colonel Whalley's regiment	} of horse	4. Colonel Rainborough's regiment } of foot
6. Colonel Rich's regiment	}	5. Colonel Overton's regiment }
7. Colonel Fleetwood's regiment	}	6. Colonel Lilburne's regiment }
8. Colonel Harrison's regiment	}	7. Colonel Barkstead's regiment }
9. Colonel Twistleton's regiment	}	

Printed *Anno Domini* 1647.

An agreement of the people for a firm and present peace upon grounds of common right.

Having by our late labours and hazards made it appear to the world at how high a rate we value our just freedom, and God having so far owned our cause as to deliver the enemies thereof into our hands, we do now hold ourselves bound in mutual duty to each other to take the best care we can for the future to avoid both the danger of returning into a slavish condition and the chargeable remedy of another war. For as it cannot be imagined that so many of our countrymen would have opposed us in this quarrel if they had understood their own good, so may we safely promise to ourselves that when our common rights and liberties shall be cleared, their endeavours will be disappointed that seek to make themselves our masters. Since therefore our former oppressions and scarce-yet-ended troubles have been occasioned either by want of frequent national meetings in council or by rendering those meetings ineffectual, we are fully agreed and resolved to provide that hereafter our representatives be neither left to an uncertainty for the time, nor made useless to the ends for which they are intended. In order whereunto we declare:

I. That the people of England being at this day very unequally distributed by counties, cities and boroughs for the election of their deputies in Parliament, ought to be more indifferently proportioned according to the number of the inhabitants: the circumstances whereof, for number, place and manner, are to be set down before the end of this present Parliament.

II. That to prevent the many inconveniences apparently arising from the long continuance of the same persons in authority, this present Parliament be dissolved upon the last day of September, which shall be in the year of our Lord, 1648.

III. That the people do of course choose themselves a Parliament once in two years, viz. upon the first Thursday in every second March, after the manner as shall be prescribed before the end of this Parliament, to begin to sit upon the first Thursday in April following at Westminster or such other place as shall be appointed from time to time by the preceding representatives, and to continue till the last day of September then next ensuing, and no longer.

IV. That the power of this and all future representatives of this nation is inferior only to theirs who choose them, and does extend, without the consent or concurrence of any other person or persons, to the enacting, altering and repealing of laws; to the erecting and abolishing of offices and courts; to the appointing, removing and calling to account magistrates and officers of all degrees; to the making war and peace; to the treating with foreign states; and generally, to whatsoever is not expressly or impliedly reserved by the represented to themselves.

Which are as follows:

1. That matters of religion and the ways of God's worship are not at all entrusted by us to any human power, because therein we cannot remit or exceed a tittle of what our consciences dictate to be the mind of God, without wilful sin. Nevertheless the public way of instructing the nation (so it be not compulsive) is referred to their discretion.

2. That the matter of impressing and constraining any of us to serve in the wars is against our freedom; and therefore we do not allow it in our representatives; the rather, because money (the sinews of war) being always at their disposal, they can never want numbers of men apt enough to engage in any just cause.

3. That after the dissolution of this present Parliament, no person be at any time questioned for anything said or done in reference to the late public differences, otherwise than in execution of the judgements of the present representatives (or House of Commons).

4. That in all laws made or to be made, every person may be bound alike; and that no tenure, estate, charter, degree, birth or place do confer any exemption from the ordinary course of legal proceedings whereunto others are subjected.

5. That as the laws ought to be equal, so they must be good and not evidently destructive to the safety and well-being of the people.

These things we declare to be our native rights, and therefore are agreed and resolved to maintain them with our utmost possibilities against all opposition whatsoever; being compelled thereunto, not only by the examples of our ancestors – whose blood was often spent in vain for the recovery of their freedoms, suffering themselves through fraudulent accommodations to be still deluded of the fruit of their victories – but also by our own woeful experience, who having long expected and dearly earned the establishment of these certain rules of government, are yet made to depend for the settlement of our peace and freedom upon him that intended our bondage and brought a cruel war upon us.[2]

For the noble and highly honoured the freeborn people of England, in their respective counties and divisions, these.

Dear countrymen and fellow-commoners,

For your sakes, our friends, estates and lives have not been dear to us; for your safety and freedom we have cheerfully endured hard labours and run most desperate hazards. And in comparison to your peace and freedom we neither do nor ever shall value our dearest blood; and we profess our bowels are and have been troubled and our hearts pained within us in seeing and considering that you have been so long bereaved of these fruits and ends of all our labours and hazards. We cannot but sympathise with you in your miseries and oppressions. It's grief and vexation of heart to us to receive your meat or monies whilst you have no advantage, nor yet the foundations of your peace and freedom surely laid. And therefore, upon most serious considerations that your principal right most essential to your well-being is the clearness, certainty, sufficiency and freedom of your power in your representatives in Parliament; and considering that the original of most of your oppressions and miseries have been either from the obscurity and doubtfulness of the power you have committed to your representatives in your elections, or from the want of courage in those whom you have betrusted to claim and exercise their power (which might probably proceed from their uncertainty of your assistance and maintenance of their power); and minding that for this right of yours and ours we engaged our lives (for the king raised the war against you and your Parliament upon this ground: that he would not suffer your representatives to provide for your peace, safety and freedom that were then in danger, by disposing of the militia and otherwise, according to their trust); and for the maintenance and defence of that power and right of yours, we hazarded all that was dear to us. And God has borne witness to the justice of our cause.

And further minding that the only effectual means to settle a just and lasting peace to obtain remedy for all your grievances, and to prevent future oppressions, is the making clear and secure the power that you betrust to your representatives in Parliament, that they may know their trust, in the faithful execution whereof you will assist them.

Upon all these grounds we propound your joining with us in the 'Agreement' herewith sent unto you, that by virtue thereof we may have Parliaments certainly called and have the time of their sitting and ending certain and their power or trust clear and unquestionable; that hereafter they may remove your burdens and secure your rights without oppositions or obstructions, and that the foundations of your peace may be so free from uncertainty that there may be no grounds for future quarrels or contentions to occasion war and bloodshed. And we desire you would consider that as these things wherein we offer to agree with you are the fruits and ends of the victories which God has given us, so the settlement of these are the most absolute means to preserve you and your posterity from slavery, oppression, distraction and trouble. By this, those whom yourselves shall choose shall have power to restore you to, and secure you in, all your rights; and they shall be in a capacity to taste of subjection as well as rule, and so shall be equally concerned with yourselves in all they do. For they must equally suffer with you under any common burdens and partake with you in any freedoms. And by this they shall be disenabled to defraud or wrong you, when the laws shall bind all alike, without privilege or exemption. And by this your consciences shall be free from tyranny and oppression, and those occasions of endless strifes and bloody wars shall be perfectly removed. Without controversy, by your joining with us in this 'Agreement' all your particular and common grievances will be redressed forthwith without delay. The Parliament must then make your relief and common good their only study.

Now because we are earnestly desirous of the peace and good of all our countrymen (even of those that have opposed us) and would to our utmost possibility provide for perfect peace and freedom and prevent all suits, debates and contentions that may happen amongst you in relation to the late war, we have therefore inserted it into this 'Agreement' that no person shall be questionable for anything done in relation to the late public differences after the dissolution of this present Parliament, further than in execution of their judgement; that thereby all may be secure from all sufferings for what they have done, and not liable hereafter to be troubled or punished by the judgement of another Parliament, which may be to their ruin unless this 'Agreement' be joined in, whereby any Acts of Indemnity or Oblivion shall be made unalterable and you and your posterities be secure.

But if any shall inquire why we should desire to join in an agreement with the people to declare these to be our native rights, and not rather petition to the Parliament for them, the reason is evident: no Act of Parliament is or can be unalterable, and so cannot be sufficient security to save you or us harmless from what another Parliament may determine if it should be corrupted. And besides, Parliaments are to receive the extent of their power and trust from those that betrust them; and therefore the people are to declare what their power and trust is, which is the intent of this 'Agreement'. And it's to be observed that though there has formerly been many Acts of Parliament for the calling of Parliaments every year, yet you have been deprived of them and enslaved through want of them.[3] And therefore, both necessity for your security in these freedoms that are essential to your well-being, and woeful experience of the manifold miseries and distractions that have been lengthened out since the war ended through want of such a settlement, requires this 'Agreement'. And when you and we shall be joined together therein we shall readily join with you to petition the Parliament, as they are our fellow-commoners equally concerned, to join with us.

And if any shall inquire why we undertake to offer this 'Agreement', we must profess we are sensible that you have been so often deceived with declarations and remonstrances and fed with vain hopes that you have sufficient reason to abandon all confidence in any persons whatsoever from whom you have no other security of their intending your freedom than bare declaration. And therefore, as our consciences witness that in simplicity and integrity of heart we have proposed lately in 'The case of the army truly stated' your freedom and deliverance from slavery, oppression and all burdens, so we desire to give you satisfying assurance thereof by this 'Agreement', whereby the foundations of your freedoms provided in 'The case of the army' shall be settled unalterably. And we shall as faithfully proceed to, and all other most vigorous actings for your good that God shall direct and enable us unto.

And though the malice of our enemies and such as they delude would blast us by scandals, aspersing us with designs of anarchy and community, yet we hope the righteous God will, not only by this our present desire of settling an equal just government but also by directing us unto all righteous undertakings simply for public good, make our uprightness and faithfulness to the interest of all our countrymen shine forth so clearly that malice itself shall be silenced and confounded. We question not but the longing expectation of a firm peace will incite you to the most speedy joining in this 'Agreement', in the prosecution whereof, or of anything that you shall desire for public good, you may be confident you shall never want the assistance of,

Your most faithful fellow-commoners now in arms for your service.

Edmund Bear	}	Lieutenant-General's regiment
Robert Everard	}	
George Garret	}	Commissary-General's regiment
Thomas Beverley	}	
William Prior	}	Colonel Fleetwood's regiment
William Bryan	}	
Matthew Weale	}	Colonel Whalley's regiment
William Russell	}	
John Dover	}	Colonel Rich's regiment
William Hudson	}	

Agents coming from other regiments unto us have subscribed the 'Agreement' to be proposed to their respective regiments and you.

For our much honoured and truly worthy fellow-commoners and soldiers, the officers and soldiers under command of his Excellency Sir Thomas Fairfax.
Gentlemen and fellow soldiers,
The deep sense of many dangers and mischiefs that may befall you in relation to the late war when so ever this Parliament shall end, unless sufficient prevention be now provided, has constrained us to study the most absolute and certain means for your security. And upon most serious considerations we judge that no Act of Indemnity can sufficiently provide for your quiet, ease and safety, because (as it has formerly been) a corrupt party, chosen into the next Parliament by your enemies' means, may possibly surprise the House and make any Act of Indemnity null, seeing they cannot fail of the king's assistance and concurrence in any such actings against you that conquered him.

And by the same means, your freedom from impressing also may in a short time be taken from you, though for the present it should be granted. We apprehend no other security by which you shall be saved harmless for what you have done in the late war than a mutual agreement between the people and you that no person shall be questioned by any authority whatsoever for anything done in relation to the late public differences after the dissolution of the present House of Commons, further than in execution of their judgement; and that your native freedom from constraint to serve in war, whether domestic or foreign, shall never be subject to the power of Parliaments, or any other. And for this end we propound the 'Agreement' that we herewith send to you to be forthwith subscribed.

And because we are confident that in judgement and conscience you hazarded your lives for the settlement of such a just and equal government that you and your posterities and all the freeborn people of this nation might enjoy justice and freedom; and that you are really sensible that the distractions, oppressions and miseries of the nation, and your want of your arrears, do proceed from the want of the establishment both of such certain rules of just government and foundations of peace as are the price of blood and the expected fruits of all the people's cost; therefore in this 'Agreement' we have inserted the certain rules of equal government under which the nation may enjoy all its rights and freedoms securely. And as we doubt not but your love to the freedom and lasting peace of the yet-distracted country will cause you to join together in this 'Agreement'.

So we question not but every true Englishman that loves the peace and freedom of England will concur with us. And then your arrears and constant pay (while you continue in arms) will certainly be brought in, out of the abundant love of the people to you; and then shall the mouths of those be stopped that scandalise you and us as endeavouring anarchy or to rule by the sword; and then will so firm an union be made between the people and you that neither any homebred or foreign enemies will dare to disturb our happy peace.

We shall add no more but this: that the knowledge of your union in laying this foundation of peace, this 'Agreement', is much longed for by,

Yours, and the people's most faithful servants.

POSTSCRIPT

Gentlemen,

We desire you may understand the reason of our extracting some principles of common freedom out of those many things proposed to you in 'The case of the army truly stated' and drawing them up into the form of an agreement. It's chiefly because for these things we first engaged against the king. He would not permit the people's representatives to provide for the nation's safety (by disposing of the militia, and other ways, according to their trust) but raised a war against them; and we engaged for the defence of that power and right of the people in their representatives. Therefore these things in the 'Agreement', the people are to claim as their native right and price of their blood, which you are obliged absolutely to procure for them.

And these being the foundations of freedom, it's necessary that they should be settled unalterably, which can be by no means but this 'Agreement' with the people.

And we cannot but remind you that the ease of the people in all their grievances depends upon the settling those principles or rules of equal government for a free people; and, were but this 'Agreement' established, doubtless all the grievances of the army and people would be redressed immediately and all things propounded in your 'Case of the army' to be insisted on, would be forthwith granted.

Then should the House of Commons have power to help the

oppressed people, which they are now bereaved of by the chief oppressors; and then they shall be equally concerned with you and all the people in the settlement of the most perfect freedom: for they shall equally suffer with you under any burdens or partake in any freedom.

We shall only add that the sum of all the 'Agreement' which we herewith offer to you is but in order to the fulfilling of our declaration of June 14 wherein we promised to the people that we would with our lives vindicate and clear their right and power in their Parliaments.

Edmund Bear	}	Lieutenant-General's regiment
Robert Everard	}	
George Garret	}	Commissary-General's regiment
Thomas Beverley	}	
William Prior	}	Colonel Fleetwood's regiment
William Bryan	}	
Matthew Weale	}	Colonel Whalley's regiment
William Russell	}	
John Dover	}	Colonel Rich's regiment
William Hudson	}	

Agents coming from other regiments unto us have subscribed the 'Agreement' to be proposed to their respective regiments and you.

EXTRACTS FROM 'THE PUTNEY DEBATES'

October–November 1647

Army headquarters had been situated at Putney since August 1647, and from September weekly meetings of the General Council were held in Putney church. This, then, was the setting on 28 October when a delegation of agents and civilians arrived at the church. However, and unbeknown to the council, they came not to discuss 'The case of the army' but the 'Agreement of the people'.

At the General Council of the Army at Putney, 28 October 1647.

The Officers being met, first said

Lieutenant-General Oliver Cromwell: That the meeting was for public businesses; those that had anything to say concerning the public business, they might have liberty to speak. [. . .]

Edward Sexby:[1] I was desired by the lieutenant-general to know the bottom of the agents' desires. They gave us this answer: that they would willingly draw them up and represent them unto you. They are come at this time to tender them to your considerations, with their resolutions to maintain them.

We have been by providence put upon strange things, such as the ancientest here do scarce remember. The army acting to these ends, providence has been with us, and yet we have found little fruit of our endeavours. The kingdom and army calls for expedition. And really I think all here, both great and small, both officers and soldiers, we may say we have leaned on, and gone to Egypt for help. The kingdom's cause requires expedition, and truly our miseries (with our fellow soldiers') cry out for present help. I think, at this time, this is your business, and I think it is in all your hearts to relieve the one and satisfy the other. You resolved if anything reasonable should be propounded to you, you would join and go along with us.

The cause of our misery is upon two things. We sought to satisfy all men, and it was well; but in going about to do it we have dissatisfied all men. We have laboured to please a king, and I think, except we go about to cut all our throats, we shall not please him; and we have gone to support an house which will prove rotten studs – I mean the Parliament, which consists of a company of rotten members. And therefore we beseech you that you will take these things into your consideration.

I shall speak to the lieutenant-general and commissary-general concerning one thing. Your credits and reputation have been much blasted, upon these two considerations. The one is for seeking to settle this kingdom in such a way wherein we thought to have satisfied all men, and we have dissatisfied them – I mean in relation to the king. The other is in reference to a Parliamentary authority, which most here would lose their lives for – to see those powers to which we will subject ourselves, loyally called. These two things are, as I think conscientiously, the cause of all those blemishes that have been cast upon either the one or the other. You are convinced God will have you to act on. But only consider how you shall act, and take those ways that will secure you and the whole kingdom. I desire you will consider those things that shall be offered to you; and, if you see anything of reason, you will join with us, that the kingdom may be eased and our fellow soldiers may be quieted in spirit. These things I have represented as my thoughts. I desire your pardon.

Cromwell: I think it is good for us to proceed to our business in some order, and that will be if we consider some things that are lately past. There has been a book printed, called 'The case of the army truly stated', and that has been taken into consideration, and there has been somewhat drawn up by way of exception to things contained in that book. And I suppose there was an answer brought to that which was taken by way of exception, and yesterday the gentleman that brought the answer,[2] he was dealt honestly and plainly withal, and he was told that there were new designs adriving, and nothing would be a clearer discovery of the sincerity of their intentions than their willingness, that were active, to bring what they had to say to be judged of by the general officers and by this General Council, that we might discern what the intentions were. Now it seems there be divers that are come hither to manifest those intentions, according to what was offered yesterday; and truly I think that the best way of our proceeding will be to receive what they have to offer. [. . .]

Buff-Coat:[3] May it please your Honour: I desired to give you satisfaction in that there was such a willingness that we might have a conference. Whereupon I did engage that interest that was in me that I would procure some to come hither, both of the soldiers and of others for assistance. And in order thereunto, here are two soldiers[4] sent from the agents, and two of our friends also,[5] to present this to your considerations, and desire your advice. According to my expectations and your engagements, you are resolved every one to purchase our inheritances which have been lost, and free this nation from the tyranny that lies upon us. I question not but that it is all your desires. And for that purpose we desire to do nothing but what we present to your consideration. And if you conceive that it must be for us to be instruments (that we might shelter ourselves like wise men before the storm comes), we desire that all carping upon words might be laid aside, and that you may fall directly upon the matter presented to you.

We have here met on purpose, according to my engagement, that whatsoever may be thought to be necessary for our satisfaction, for the right understanding one of another, might be done, that we might go on together. For, though our ends and aims be the same, if one thinks this way, another another way, that way which is the best for the subject is that they both may be hearkened unto.

[*'An agreement of the people' read.*]

Buff-Coat: For the privileges here demanded, I think it will be strange that we that are soldiers cannot have them for ourselves, if not for the whole kingdom; and therefore we beseech you consider of it.

Cromwell: These things that you have now offered, they are new to us: they are things that we have not at all (at least in this method and thus circumstantially) had any opportunity to consider of, because they came to us but thus, as you see; this is the first time we had a view of them.

Truly this paper does contain in it very great alterations of the very government of the kingdom, alterations from that government that it has been under, I believe I may almost say, since it was a nation – I say, I think I may almost say so. And what the consequences of such an alteration as this would be, if there were nothing else to be considered, wise men and godly men ought to consider. I say, if there were nothing else to be considered but the very weight and nature of the things contained in this paper. Therefore, although the pretensions in it, and the expressions in it, are very plausible, and if we could leap out of one condition into another that had so specious things in it as this has, I suppose there would not be much dispute – though perhaps some of these things may be very well disputed. How do we know if, whilst we are disputing these things, another company of men shall not gather together, and put out a paper as plausible perhaps as this? I do not know why it might not be done by that time you have agreed upon this, or got hands to it if that be the way. And not only another, and another, but many of this kind. And if so, what do you think the consequence of that would be? Would it not be confusion? Would it not be utter confusion? Would it not make England like the Switzerland country, one canton of the Swiss against another, and one county against another? I ask you whether it be not fit for every honest man seriously to lay that upon his heart? And if so, what would that produce but an absolute desolation – an absolute desolation to the nation – and we in the meantime tell the nation, 'It is for your liberty; 'tis for your privilege; 'tis for your good.' Pray God it prove so, whatsoever course we run. But truly, I think we are not only to consider what the consequences are if there were nothing else but this paper, but we are to consider the probability of the ways and means to accomplish the thing proposed: that is to say, whether, according to reason and judgement, the spirits and temper of the people of this nation are prepared to receive and to go on along with it, and whether those great difficulties that lie in our way are in a likelihood to be either overcome or removed. Truly, to anything that's good, there's no doubt on it, objections may be made and framed; but let every honest man consider whether or no there be not very real objections to this in point of difficulty. I know a man may answer all difficulties with faith, and faith will answer all difficulties really where it is, but we are very apt, all of us, to call that faith, that perhaps may be but carnal imagination, and carnal reasonings. Give me leave to say this: there will be very great mountains in the way of this, if this were the thing in present con-sideration; and, therefore, we ought to consider the consequences, and God has given us our reason that we may do this. It is not enough to propose things that are good in the end, but suppose this model were an excellent model, and fit for England and the kingdom to receive, it is our duty as Christians and men to consider consequences, and to consider the way. [. . .]

First of all there is the question what obligations lie upon us and how far we are engaged. This ought to be our consideration and yours, saving that in this you have the advantage of us – you that are the soldiers you have not, but you that are not soldiers – you reckon yourselves at a loose and at a liberty, as men that have no obligation upon you. Perhaps we conceive we have; and therefore this is that I may say, both to those that come with you, and to my fellow officers and all others that hear me: that it concerns us as we would approve ourselves before God, and before men that are able to judge of us, if we do not make good our engagements, if we do not make good that that the world expects we should make good. I do not speak to determine what that is; but if I be not much mistaken, we have in the time of our danger issued out declarations; we have been required by the Parliament, because our declarations were general, to declare particularly what we meant. And (having done that) how far that obliges or not obliges us, that is by us to be considered – if we mean honestly and sincerely and to approve ourselves to God as honest men. And therefore, having heard this paper read, this remains to us: that we again review what we have engaged in, and what we have that lies upon us. He that departs from that that is a real engagement and a real tie upon him, I think he transgresses without faith; for faith will bear up men in every honest obligation, and God does expect from men the performance of every honest obligation. And therefore I have no more to say but this: we having received your paper, we shall amongst ourselves consider what to do; and before we take this into consideration, it is fit for us to consider how far we are obliged, and how far we are free; and I hope we shall prove ourselves honest men where we are free to tender anything to the good of the public. And this is that I thought good to offer to you upon this paper.

John Wildman: Being yesterday at a meeting where divers country gentlemen and soldiers and others were, and amongst the rest the agents of the five regiments, and having weighed their papers, I must freely confess I did declare my agreement with them. Upon that, they were pleased to declare their sense in most particulars of their proceedings, to me, and desired me that I would be their mouth, and in their names represent their sense unto you. And upon that ground I shall speak something in answer to that which your Honour last spoke.

I shall not reply anything at present, till it come to be further debated, either concerning the consequences of what is propounded, or the contents of this paper; but I conceive the chief weight of your Honour's speech lay in this: that you were first to consider what obligations lay upon you, and how far you were engaged, before you could consider what was just in this paper now propounded; adding that God would protect men in keeping honest promises. To that I must only offer this. That, according to the best knowledge I have of their apprehensions, they do apprehend that whatever obligation is past must afterwards be considered when it is urged whether the engagement were honest and just or no; and if it were not just it does not oblige the persons, if it be an oath itself. But if, while there is not so clear a light, any person passes an engagement, it is judged by them (and I so judge it) to be an act of honesty for that man to recede from his former judgement, and to abhor it. And therefore I conceive the first thing is to consider the honesty of what is offered; otherwise it cannot be considered of any obligation that does prepossess. By the consideration of the justice of what is offered, that obligation shall appear whether it was just or no. If it were not just, I cannot but be confident of the searings of your consciences. And I conceive this to be their sense; and upon this account, upon a more serious review of all declarations past, they see no obligations which are just, that they contradict by proceeding in this way.

Commissary-General Henry Ireton: Sure this gentleman has not been acquainted with our engagements. For he that will cry out of breach of engagement in slight and trivial things and things necessitated to, I can hardly think that man that is so tender of an engagement as to frame, or at least concur with, this book, 'The case of the army', in their insisting upon every punctilio of the army's engagement, can be of that principle that no engagement is binding further than that he thinks it just or no. For he hints that, if he that makes an engagement (be it what it will be) have further light that this engagement was not good or honest, then he is free from it. Truly, if the sense were put thus, that a man finds he has entered into an engagement and thinks that it was not a just engagement, I confess something might be said that such a man might declare himself for his part ready to suffer some penalty upon his person or upon his party. The question is, whether it be an engagement to another party. Now if a man venture into an engagement from himself to another, and find that engagement not just and honest, he must apply himself to the other party and say: 'I cannot actively perform it; I will make you amends as near as I can.' Upon the same ground men are not obliged to be obedient to any authority that is set up, though it were this authority that is proposed here – I am not engaged to be so actively to that authority. Yet if I have engaged that they shall bind me by law, though afterwards I find they do require me to a thing that is not just or honest, I am bound so far to my engagement that I must submit and suffer, though I cannot act and do that which their laws do impose upon me. If that caution were put in where a performance of an engagement might be expected from another, and he could not do it because he thought it was not honest to be performed, if such a thing were put into the case, it is possible there might be some reason for it. But to take it as it is delivered in general, that we are free to break, if it subsequently appear unjust, whatever engagement we have entered into, though it be a promise of something to another party, wherein that other party is concerned, wherein he has a benefit if we make it good, wherein he has a prejudice if we make it not good: this is a principle that will take away all commonwealths, and will take away the fruit of this very engagement if it were entered into; and men of this principle would think themselves as little as may be obliged by any law if in their apprehensions it be not a good law. I think they would think themselves as little obliged to think of standing to that authority that is proposed in this 'Agreement'. [. . .]

Colonel Thomas Rainborough:[6] [. . .] I shall speak my mind, that, whoever he be that has done this, he has done it with much respect to the good of his country. It is said, there are many plausible things in it. Truly, many things have engaged me, which, if I had not known they should have been nothing but good, I would not have engaged in. It has been said, that if a man be engaged he must perform his engagements. I am wholly confident that every honest man is bound in duty to God and his conscience, let him be engaged in what he will, to decline it when he sees it to be evil: he is engaged, and as clearly convinced, to discharge his duty to God as ever he was for it. And that I shall make good out of the scripture, and clear it by that, if that be anything.

There are two further objections are made against it: the one is division. Truly I think we are utterly undone if we divide, but I hope that honest things have carried us on thus long, and will keep us together, and I hope that we shall not divide. Another thing is difficulties. Oh, unhappy men are we that ever began this war! If ever we had looked upon difficulties, I do not know that ever we should have looked an enemy in the face. Truly, I think the Parliament were very indiscreet to contest with the king if they did not consider first that they should go through difficulties; and I think there was no man that entered into this war, that did not engage to go through difficulties. And I shall humbly offer unto you – it may be the last time I shall offer, it may be so, but I shall discharge my conscience in it – it is this. That truly I think, let the difficulties be round about you – have you death before you, the sea on each side of you and behind you – and are you convinced that the thing is just, I think you are bound in conscience to carry it on; and I think at the last day it can never be answered to God, that you did not do it. For I think it is a poor service to God and the kingdom, to take their pay and to decline the work. I hear it said that it's a huge alteration, it's a bringing in of new laws, and that this kingdom has been under this government ever since it was a kingdom. If writings be true there have been many scufflings between the honest men of England and those that have tyrannised over them; and if it be true what I have read, there is none of those just and equitable laws that the people of England are born to, but are entrenchments on the once enjoyed privileges of their rulers altogether. But even if they were those which the people have been always under, if the people find that they are not suitable to free men as they are, I know no reason that should deter me, either in what I must answer before God or the world, from endeavouring by all means to gain anything that might be of more advantage to them than the government under which they live. I do not press that you should go on with this thing, for I think that every man that would speak to it will be less able till he has some time to consider it. I do make it my motion: that two or three days' time may be set for every man to consider, and that all that is to be considered is the justness of the thing – and if that be considered then all things are – so that there may be nothing to deter us from it, but that we may do that which is just to the people. [. . .]

[*In spite of Rainborough's motion, the issue of engagements – and the circumstances under which it was lawful to break them – thereafter dominated the day's debate. Eventually, a committee was appointed to examine the 'Agreement' in the light of the army's previous engagements.*]

Putney, 29 October 1647.

[*The second day's debate – deservedly the most famous – took place in the quartermaster-general's quarters following a morning prayer meeting. After the arrival of the agents and civilians, the 'Agreement' was read to the assembled audience, followed by the first article by itself.*]

[. . .] *Ireton*: The exception that lies in it is this: it is said, they are to be distributed 'according to the number of the inhabitants', 'The people of

England', etc. And this does make me think that the meaning is, that every man that is an inhabitant is to be equally considered, and to have an equal voice in the election of those representers, the persons that are for the general representative. And if that be the meaning, then I have something to say against it. But if it be only that those people that by the civil constitution of this kingdom, which is original and fundamental, and beyond which I am sure no memory of record does go –

Commissary Nicholas Cowling,[7] *interrupting*: Not before the Conquest.

Ireton: But before the Conquest it was so. If it be intended that those that by that constitution that was before the Conquest, that has been beyond memory, such persons that have been before under that constitution the electors, should be still the electors, I have no more to say against it. [. . .]

Ireton asked: Whether those men whose hands are to the 'Agreement', or those that brought it, do know so much of the matter as to know whether they mean that all that had a former right of election are to be electors, or that those that had no right before are to come in.

Cowling: In the time before the Conquest, and since the Conquest, the greatest part of the kingdom was in vassalage.

Maximilian Petty: We judge that all inhabitants that have not lost their birthright should have an equal voice in elections.

Rainborough: I desired that those that had engaged in it might be included. For really I think that the poorest he that is in England has a life to live, as the greatest he; and therefore truly, sir, I think it's clear, that every man that is to live under a government ought first by his own consent to put himself under that government; and I do think that the poorest man in England is not at all bound in a strict sense to that government that he has not had a voice to put himself under; and I am confident that, when I have heard the reasons against it, something will be said to answer those reasons, in so much that I should doubt whether he was an Englishman or no, that should doubt of these things.

Ireton: That's the meaning of this, 'according to the number of the inhabitants'?

Give me leave to tell you, that if you make this the rule I think you must fly for refuge to an absolute natural right, and you must deny all civil right; and I am sure it will come to that in the consequence. This, I perceive, is pressed as that which is so essential and due: the right of the people of this kingdom, and as they are the people of this kingdom, distinct and divided from other people, and that we must for this right lay aside all other considerations. This is so just, this is so due, this is so right to them; and that those that they do thus choose must have such a power of binding all, and loosing all, according to those limitations. This is pressed as so due, and so just, as it is argued, that it is an engagement paramount to all others, and you must for it lay aside all others; if you have engaged any otherwise, you must break it. We must so look upon these as thus held out to us; so it was held out by the gentleman that brought it yesterday.

For my part, I think it is no right at all. I think that no person has a right to an interest or share in the disposing of the affairs of the kingdom, and in determining or choosing those that shall determine what laws we shall be ruled by here, no person has a right to this, that has not a permanent fixed interest in this kingdom, and those persons together are properly the represented of this kingdom, and consequently are also to make up the representers of this kingdom, who taken together do comprehend whatsoever is of real or permanent interest in the kingdom.[8] And I am sure otherwise I cannot tell what any man can say why a foreigner coming in amongst us – or as many as will coming in amongst us, or by force or otherwise settling themselves here, or at least by our permission having a being here – why they should not as well lay claim to it as any other.

We talk of birthright: truly by birthright there is thus much claim. Men may justly have by birthright, by their very being born in England, that we should not seclude them out of England, that we should not refuse to give them air and place and ground, and the freedom of the highways and other things, to live amongst us – not any man that is born here, though by his birth there come nothing at all (that is part of the permanent interest of this kingdom) to him. That I think is due to a man by birth. But that by a man's being born here he shall have a share in that power that shall dispose of the lands here, and of all things here, I do not think it a sufficient ground.

I am sure if we look upon that which is the utmost (within any man's view) of what was originally the constitution of this kingdom, upon that which is most radical and fundamental, and which if you take away, there is no man has any land, any goods, or any civil interest, that is this: that those that choose the representers for the making of laws by which this state and kingdom are to be governed, are the persons who, taken together, do comprehend the local interest of this kingdom; that is, the persons in whom all land lies, and those in corporations in whom all trading lies. This is the most fundamental constitution of this kingdom and that which if you do not allow, you allow none at all. This constitution has limited and determined it that only those shall have voices in elections. It is true, as was said by a gentleman near me, the meanest man in England ought to have a voice in the election of the government he lives under – but only if he has some local interest. I say this: that those that have the meanest local interest, that man that has but forty shillings a year, he has as great a voice in the election of a knight for the shire as he that has ten thousand a year, or more if he had never so much; and therefore there is that regard had to it. But this local interest, still the constitution of this government has had an eye to (and what other government has not an eye to this?). It does not relate to the interest of the kingdom if it do not lay the foundation of the power that's given to the representers in those who have a permanent and a local interest in the kingdom, and who taken all together do comprehend the whole interest of the kingdom.

There is all the reason and justice that can be, in this: if I will come to live in a kingdom, being a foreigner to it, or live in a kingdom, having no permanent interest in it, and if I will desire as a stranger, or claim as one freeborn here, the air, the free passage of highways, the protection of laws, and all such things – if I will either desire them or claim them, then I (if I have no permanent interest in that kingdom) must submit to those laws and those rules which they shall choose, who, taken together, do comprehend the whole interest of the kingdom. And if we shall go to take away this, we shall plainly go to take away all property and interest that any man has either in land by inheritance, or in estate by possession, or anything else – I say, if you take away this fundamental part of the civil constitution.

Rainborough: Truly, sir, I am of the same opinion I was, and am resolved to keep it till I know reason why I should not. I confess my memory is bad, and therefore I am fain to make use of my pen. I remember that, in a former speech which this gentleman brought before this meeting, he was saying that in some cases he should not value whether there were a king or no king, whether Lords or no Lords, whether a property or no property. For my part I differ in that. I do very much care whether there be a king or no king, Lords or no Lords, property or no property; and I think, if we do not all take care, we shall all have none of these very shortly.

But as to this present business, I do hear nothing at all that can convince me why any man that is born in England ought not to have his voice in election of burgesses. It is said that if a man have not a permanent interest, he can have no claim; and that we must be no freer than the laws will let us be, and that there is no law in any chronicle will let us be freer than that we now enjoy. Something was said to this yesterday. I do think that the main cause why Almighty God gave men reason, it was that they should make use of that reason, and that they should improve it for that end and purpose that God gave it them. And truly, I think that half a loaf is better than none if a man be hungry. This gift of reason without other property may seem a small thing, yet I think there is nothing that God has given a man that anyone else can take from him. And therefore I say, that either it must be the law of God or the law of man that must prohibit the meanest man in the kingdom to have this benefit as well as the greatest. I do not find anything in the law of God, that a lord shall choose twenty burgesses, and a gentleman but two, or a poor man shall choose none: I find no such thing in the law of nature, nor in the law of nations. But I do find that all Englishmen must be subject to English laws, and I do verily believe that there is no man but will say that the foundation of all law lies in the people, and if it lie in the people, I am to seek for this exemption.

And truly I have thought something else: in what a miserable distressed condition would many a man that has fought for the Parliament in this quarrel be! I will be bound to say that many a man whose zeal and affection to God and this kingdom has carried him forth in this cause, has so spent his estate that, in the way the state and the army are going, he shall not hold up his head, if when his estate is lost, and not worth forty shillings a year, a man shall not have any interest. And there are many other ways by which the estates men have (if that be the rule which God in his providence does use) do fall to decay. A man, when he has an estate, has an interest in making laws, but when he has none, he has no power in it; so that a man cannot lose that which he has for the maintenance of his family but he must also lose that which God and nature has given him! And therefore I do think, and am still of the same opinion, that every man born in England cannot, ought not, neither by the law of God nor the law of nature, to be exempted from the choice of those who are to make laws for him to live under, and for him, for all I know, to lose his life under. And therefore I think there can be no great stick in this.

Truly I think that there is not this day reigning in England a greater fruit or effect of tyranny than this very thing would produce. Truly I know nothing free but only the knight of the shire, nor do I know anything in a Parliamentary way that is clear from the height and fullness of tyranny, but only that. As for this of corporations which you also mentioned, it is as contrary to freedom as may be. For, sir, what is it? The king he grants a patent under the Broad-Seal of England to such a corporation to send burgesses, he grants to such a city to send burgesses. When a poor base corporation from the king's grant shall send two burgesses, when five hundred men of estate shall not send one, when those that are to make their laws are called by the king, or cannot act but by such a call, truly I think that the people of England have little freedom.

Ireton: I think there was nothing that I said to give you occasion to think that I did contend for this, that such a corporation as that should have the electing of a man to the Parliament. I think I agreed to this matter, that all should be equally distributed.[9] But the question is, whether it should be distributed to all persons, or whether the same persons that are the electors now should be the electors still, and it be equally distributed amongst them. I do not see anybody else that makes this objection; and if nobody else be sensible of it I shall soon have done. Only I shall a little crave your leave to represent the consequences of it, and clear myself from one thing that was misrepresented by the gentleman that sat next me. I think, if the gentleman remember himself, he cannot but remember that what I said was to this effect: that if I saw the hand of God leading so far as to destroy king, and destroy Lords, and destroy property, and leave no such thing at all amongst us, I should acquiesce in it; and so I did not care, if no king, no Lords, or no property should be, in comparison of the tender care that I have of the honour of God, and of the people of God, whose good name is so much concerned in this army. This I did deliver so, and not absolutely.

All the main thing that I speak for, is because I would have an eye to property. I hope we do not come to contend for victory, but let every man consider with himself that he do not go that way to take away all property. For here is the case of the most fundamental part of the constitution of the kingdom, which if you take away, you take away all by that. Here men of this and this quality are determined to be the electors of men to the Parliament, and they are all those who have any permanent interest in the kingdom, and who, taken together, do comprehend the whole permanent, local interest of the kingdom. I mean by permanent and local, that it is not able to be removed anywhere else. As for instance, he that has a freehold, and that freehold cannot be removed out of the kingdom; and so there's a freeman of a corporation, a place which has the privilege of a market and trading, which if you should allow to all places equally, I do not see how you could preserve any peace in the kingdom, and that is the reason why in the constitution we have but some few market towns. Now those people that have freeholds and those that are the freemen of corporations, were looked upon by the former constitution to comprehend the permanent interest of the kingdom. For first, he that has his livelihood by his trade, and by his freedom of trading in such a corporation, which he cannot exercise in another, he is tied to that place, for his livelihood depends upon it. And secondly, that man has an interest, has a permanent interest there, upon which he may live, and live a freeman without dependence. These things the constitution of this kingdom has looked at.

Now I wish we may all consider of what right you will challenge that all the people should have right to elections. Is it by the right of nature? If you will hold forth that as your ground, then I think you must deny all property too, and this is my reason. For thus: by that same right of nature (whatever it be) that you pretend, by which you can say, one man has an equal right with another to the choosing of him that shall govern him, by the same right of nature, he has the same equal right in any goods he sees – meat, drink, clothes – to take and use them for his sustenance. He has a freedom to the land, to take the ground, to exercise it, till it; he has the same freedom to anything that anyone does account himself to have any propriety in. Why now I say then, if you, against the most fundamental part of the civil constitution (which I have now declared), will plead the law of nature, that a man should (paramount to this, and contrary to this) have a power of choosing those men that shall determine what shall be law in this state, though he himself have no permanent interest in the state, but whatever interest he has he may carry about with him, if this be allowed because by the right of nature we are free, we are equal, one man must have as much voice as another, then show me what step or difference there is, why I may not by the same right take your property, though not of necessity to sustain nature. It is for my better being, and the better settlement of the kingdom? Possibly not for it, neither: possibly I may not have so real a regard to the peace of the kingdom as that man who has a permanent interest in it. He that is here today, and gone tomorrow, I do not see that he has such a permanent interest. Since you cannot plead to it by anything but the law of nature, or for anything but for the end of better being, and since that better being is not certain, and what is more, destructive to another; upon these grounds, if you do, paramount to all constitutions, hold up this law of nature, I would fain have any man show me their bounds, where you will end, and why you should not take away all property?

Rainborough: I shall now be a little more free and open with you than I was before. I wish we were all true-hearted, and that we did all carry ourselves with integrity. If I did mistrust you I would not use such asseverations. I think it does go on mistrust, and things are thought too readily matters of reflection, that were never intended. For my part, as I think, you forgot something that was in my speech, and you do not only yourselves believe that some men are inclining to anarchy, but you would make all men believe that. And, sir, to say because a man pleads that every man has a voice by right of nature, that therefore it destroys by the same argument all property, this is to forget the law of God. That there's a property, the law of God says it; else why has God made that law, 'Thou shall not steal'? I am a poor man, therefore I must be oppressed: if I have no interest in the kingdom, I must suffer by all their laws, be they right or wrong. Thus: a gentleman lives in a county and has three or four lordships, as some men have (God knows how they got them); and when a Parliament is called he must be a Parliament-man; and it may be he sees some poor men, they live near this man, he can crush them – I have known an invasion to make sure he has turned the poor men out of doors; and I would fain know whether the potency of rich men do not this, and so keep them under the greatest tyranny that was ever thought of in the world. And therefore I think that to that it is fully answered: God has set down that thing as to propriety with this law of his, 'Thou shall not steal'. And for my part I am against any such thought, and, as for yourselves, I wish you would not make the world believe that we are for anarchy.

Cromwell: I know nothing but this, that they that are the most yielding have the greatest wisdom. But really, sir, this is not right as it should be. No man says that you have a mind to anarchy, but that the consequence of this rule tends to anarchy, must end in anarchy; for where is there any bound or limit set if you take away this limit, that men that have no interest but the interest of breathing shall have no voice in elections? Therefore I am confident on it, we should not be so hot one with another.

Rainborough: I know that some particular men we debate with believe we are for anarchy.

Ireton: I profess I must clear myself as to that point. I would not desire, I cannot allow myself, to lay the least scandal upon anybody. And truly, for that gentleman that did take so much offence, I do not know why he should take it so. We speak to the paper – not to persons – and to the matter of the paper. And I hope that no man is so much engaged to the matter of the paper: I hope that our persons, and our hearts and judgements, are not so pinned to papers but that we are ready to hear what good or ill consequence will flow from it.

I have, with as much plainness and clearness of reason as I could, showed you how I did conceive the doing of this that the paper advocates takes away that which is the most original, the most funda-mental civil constitution of this kingdom, and which is, above all, that constitution by which I have any property. If you will take away that and set up, as a thing paramount, whatever a man may claim by the law of nature, though it be not a thing of necessity to him for the sustenance of nature, if you do make this your rule, I desire clearly to understand where then remains property.

Now then, I would misrepresent nothing the answer which had anything of matter in it, the great and main answer upon which that which has been said against this objection rests, seemed to be that it will not make a breach of property, for this reason: that there is a law, 'Thou shall not steal'. But the same law says, 'Honour thy father and thy mother', and that law does likewise hold out that it does extend to all that (in that place where we are in) are our governors; so that by that there is a forbidding of breaking a civil law when we may live quietly under it, and that by a divine law. Again it is said – indeed was said before – that there is no law, no divine law, that tells us that such a corporation must have the election of burgesses, such a shire of knights, or the like. Divine law extends not to particular things. And so, on the other side, if a man were to demonstrate his right to property by divine law, it would be very remote. Our right to property descends from other things, as also does our right of sending burgesses. That divine law does not determine particulars but generals in relation to man and man, and to property, and all things else; and we should be as far to seek if we should go to prove a property in a thing by divine law, as to prove that I have an interest in choosing burgesses of the Parliament by divine law. And truly, under favour, I refer it to all, whether there be anything of solution to that objection that I made, if it be understood – I submit it to any man's judgement.

Rainborough: To the thing itself – property in the franchise – I would fain know how it comes to be the property of some men, and not of others. As for estates and those kind of things, and other things that belong to men, it will be granted that they are property; but I deny that that is a property, to a lord, to a gentleman, to any man more than another in the kingdom of England. If it be a property, it is a property by a law, and I think that there is very little property in this thing by the law of the land, because I think that the law of the land in that thing is the most tyrannical law under heaven. And I would fain know what we have fought for: for our laws and liberties? And this is the old law of England – and that which enslaves the people of England – that they should be bound by laws in which they have no voice at all! With respect to the divine law which says, 'Honour thy father and thy mother', the great dispute is, who is a right father and a right mother? I am bound to know who is my father and mother; and – I take it in the same sense you do – I would have a distinction, a character whereby God commands me to honour them. And for my part I look upon the people of England so, that wherein they have not voices in the choosing of their governors – their civil fathers and mothers – they are not bound to that command- ment.

Petty: I desire to add one word concerning the word 'property'. It is for something that anarchy is so much talked of. For my own part I cannot believe in the least that it can be clearly derived from that paper. 'Tis true, that somewhat may be derived in the paper against the king, the power of the king, and somewhat against the power of the Lords; and the truth is when I shall see God going about to throw down king and Lords and property, then I shall be contented. But I hope that they may live to see the power of the king and the Lords thrown down, that yet may live to see property preserved. And for this of changing the representative of the nation, of changing those that choose the representative, making of them more full, taking more into the number than formerly, I had verily thought we had all agreed in it that more should have chosen – all that had desired a more equal representation than we now have. For now those only choose who have forty shillings freehold. A man may have a lease for one hundred pounds a year, a man may have a lease for three lives, but he has no voice. But as for this argument, that it destroys all right to property that every Englishman that is an inhabitant of England should choose and have a voice in the representatives, I suppose it is, on the contrary, the only means to preserve all property. For I judge every

man is naturally free; and I judge the reason why men chose representatives when they were in so great numbers that every man could not
give his voice directly, was that they who were chosen might preserve
property for all; and therefore men agreed to come into some form of
government that they might preserve property, and I would fain know, if
we were to begin a government, whether you would say, 'You have not
forty shillings a year, therefore you shall not have a voice.' Whereas
before there was a government every man had such a voice, and
afterwards, and for this very cause, they did choose representatives,
and put themselves into forms of government that they may preserve
property, and therefore it is not to destroy it, to give every man a voice.

Ireton: I think we shall not be so apt to come to a right understanding
in this business, if one man, and another man, and another man do speak
their several thoughts and conceptions to the same purpose, as if we do
consider where the objection lies, and what the answer is which is made
to it; and therefore I desire we may do so. To that which this gentleman
spoke last, the main thing that he seemed to answer was this: that he
would make it appear that the going about to establish this government,
or such a government, is not a destruction of property, nor does not tend
to the destruction of property, because the people's falling into a
government is for the preservation of property. What weight there is
in it lies in this: since there is a falling into a government, and
government is to preserve property, therefore this cannot be against
property. The objection does not lie in that, the making of the
representation more equal, but in the introducing of men into an
equality of interest in this government, who have no property in this
kingdom, or who have no local permanent interest in it. For if I had said
that I would not wish at all that we should have any enlargement of the
bounds of those that are to be the electors, then you might have excepted
against it. But what I said was that I would not go to enlarge it beyond all
bounds, so that upon the same ground you may admit of so many men
from foreign states as would outvote you: the objection lies still in this. I
do not mean that I would have it restrained to that proportion that now
obtains, but to restrain it still to men who have a local, a permanent
interest in the kingdom, who have such an interest that they may live
upon it as free men, and who have such an interest as is fixed upon a
place, and is not the same equally everywhere. If a man be an inhabitant
upon a rack rent for a year, for two years, or twenty years, you cannot
think that man has any fixed permanent interest. That man, if he pay the

rent that his land is worth, and has no advantage but what he has by his land, is as good a man, may have as much interest, in another kingdom as here. I do not speak of not enlarging this representation at all, but of keeping this to the most fundamental constitution in this kingdom: that is, that no person that has not a local and permanent interest in the kingdom should have an equal dependence in election with those that have. But if you go beyond this law, if you admit any man that has a breath and being, I did show you how this will destroy property. It may come to destroy property thus. You may have such men chosen, or at least the major part of them, as have no local and permanent interest. Why may not those men vote against all property? Again you may admit strangers by this rule, if you admit them once to inhabit, and those that have interest in the land may be voted out of their land. It may destroy property that way. But here is the rule that you go by. You infer this to be the right of the people, of every inhabitant, because man has such a right in nature, though it be not of necessity for the preserving of his being; and therefore you are to overthrow the most fundamental constitution for this. By the same rule, show me why you will not, by the same right of nature, make use of anything that any man has, though it be not for the necessary sustenance of men. Show me what you will stop at, wherein you will fence any man in a property by this rule.

Rainborough: I desire to know how this comes to be a property in some men, and not in others.

Colonel Nathaniel Rich:[10] I confess there is weight in that objection that the commissary-general last insisted upon; for you have five to one in this kingdom that have no permanent interest. Some men have ten, some twenty servants, some more, some less; if the master and servant shall be equal electors, then clearly those that have no interest in the kingdom will make it their interest to choose those that have no interest. It may happen, that the majority may by law, not in a confusion, destroy property; there may be a law enacted, that there shall be an equality of goods and estate. I think that either of the extremes may be urged to inconveniency; that is, that men that have no interest as to estate should have no interest as to election and that they should have an equal interest. But there may be a more equitable division and distribution than that he that has nothing should have an equal voice; and certainly there may be some other way thought of, that there may be a representative of the poor as well as the rich, and not to exclude all. I remember there were many workings and revolutions, as we have heard, in the Roman Senate;

and there was never a confusion that did appear (and that indeed was come to) till the state came to know this kind of distribution of election. That is how the people's voices were bought and sold, and that by the poor; and thence it came that he that was the richest man, and a man of some considerable power among the soldiers, and one they resolved on, made himself a perpetual dictator. And if we strain too far to avoid monarchy in kings let us take heed that we do not call for emperors to deliver us from more than one tyrant.

Rainborough: I should not have spoken again. I think it is a fine gilded pill. But there is much danger, and it may seem to some that there is some kind of remedy possible. I think that we are better as we are if it can be really proved that the poor shall choose many and still the people be in the same case, be over-voted still. But of this, and much else, I am unsatisfied, and therefore truly, sir, I should desire to go close to the business; and the first thing that I am unsatisfied in is how it comes about that there is such a propriety in some freeborn Englishmen, and not in others.

Cowling: Whether the younger son have not as much right to the inheritance as the eldest?[11]

Ireton: Will you decide it by the light of nature?

Cowling: Why election was given only to those with freeholds of forty shillings a year (which was then worth more than forty pounds a year now), the reason was: that the Commons of England were overpowered by the Lords, who had abundance of vassals, but that still they might make their laws good against encroaching prerogatives by this means; therefore they did exclude all slaves. Now the case is not so: all slaves have bought their freedoms, and they are more free that in the commonwealth are more beneficial. Yet there are men of substance in the country with no voice in elections. There is a tanner in Staines worth three thousand pounds, and another in Reading worth three horseskins: the second has a voice; the first, none.

Ireton: In the beginning of your speech you seem to acknowledge that by law, by civil constitution, the propriety of having voices in election was fixed in certain persons. So then your exception of your argument does not prove that by civil constitution they have no such propriety, but your argument does acknowledge that by civil constitution they have such propriety. You argue against this law only that this law is not good.

Wildman: Unless I be very much mistaken we are very much deviated from the first question. Instead of following the first proposition to inquire what is just, I conceive we look to prophecies, and look to what may be the event, and judge of the justness of a thing by the consequence. I desire we may recall ourselves to the question whether it be right or no. I conceive all that has been said against it will be reduced to this question of consequences, and to another reason, that it is against a fundamental law: that every person choosing ought to have a permanent interest, because it is not fit that those should choose Parliaments that have no lands to be disposed of by Parliament.

Ireton: If you will take it by the way, it is not fit that the representees should choose as the representers, or the persons who shall make the law in the kingdom, those who have not a permanent fixed interest in the kingdom. The reason is the same in the two cases.

Wildman: Sir, I do so take it; and I conceive that that is brought in for the same reason: that foreigners might otherwise not only come to have a voice in our elections as well as the native inhabitants, but to be elected.

Ireton: That is upon supposition that these foreigners should be all inhabitants.

Wildman: I shall begin with the last first. The case is different with the native inhabitant and the foreigner. If a foreigner shall be admitted to be an inhabitant in the nation, so he will submit to that form of government as the natives do, he has the same right as the natives but in this particular. Our case is to be considered thus: that we have been under slavery; that's acknowledged by all. Our very laws were made by our conquerors; and whereas it's spoken much of chronicles, I conceive there is no credit to be given to any of them; and the reason is because those that were our lords, and made us their vassals, would suffer nothing else to be chronicled. We are now engaged for our freedom. That's the end of Parliaments: not to constitute what is already established, but to act according to the just rules of government. Every person in England has as clear a right to elect his representative as the greatest person in England. I conceive that's the undeniable maxim of government: that all government is in the free consent of the people. If so, then upon that account there is no person that is under a just government, or has justly his own, unless he by his own free consent be put under that government. This he cannot be unless he be consenting to it, and therefore, according to this maxim, there is never a person in England but ought to have a voice in elections. If this, as that gentleman says, be true, there are no laws that in this strictness and rigour of justice any man is bound to, that are not made by those whom he does consent to. And therefore I should humbly move, that if the question be stated – which would soonest bring things to an issue – it might rather be thus: whether any person can justly be bound by law, who does not give his consent that such persons shall make laws for him?

Ireton: Let the question be so: whether a man can be bound to any law that he does not consent to? And I shall tell you, that he may and ought to be bound to a law that he does not give a consent to, nor does not choose any to consent to; and I will make it clear. If a foreigner come within this kingdom, if that stranger will have liberty to dwell here who has no local interest here, he, as a man, it's true, has air, the passage of highways, the protection of laws, and all that by nature; we must not expel him our coasts, give him no being amongst us, nor kill him because he comes upon our land, comes up our stream, arrives at our shore. It is a piece of hospitality, of humanity, to receive that man amongst us. But if that man be received to a being amongst us, I think that man may very well be content to submit himself to the law of the land; that is, the law that is made by those people that have a property, a fixed property, in the land. I think, if any man will receive protection from this people though neither he nor his ancestors, not any betwixt him and Adam, did ever give concurrence to this constitution, I think this man ought to be subject to those laws, and to be bound by those laws, so long as he continues amongst them. That is my opinion. A man ought to be subject to a law, that did not give his consent, but with this reservation: that if this man do think himself unsatisfied to be subject to this law he may go into another kingdom. And so the same reason does extend, in my understanding, to that man that has no permanent interest in the kingdom. If he has money, his money is as good in another place as here; he has nothing that does locally fix him to this kingdom. If that man will live in this kingdom, or trade amongst us, that man ought to subject himself to the law made by the people who have the interest of this kingdom in them. And yet I do acknowledge that which you take to be so general a maxim, that in every kingdom, within every land, the original of power of making laws, of determining what shall be law in the land, does lie in the people, but by the people is meant those that are possessed of the permanent interest in the land. But whoever is extraneous to this, that is, as good a man in another land, that man ought to give such a respect to the property of men that live in the land. They do not determine that I shall live in this land. Why should I have any interest in determining what shall be the law of this land?

Major William Rainborough:[12] I think if it can be made to appear that it is a just and reasonable thing, and that it is for the preservation of all the native freeborn men, that they should have an equal voice in election, I think it ought to be made good unto them. And the reason is, that the chief end of this government is to preserve persons as well as estates, and if any law shall take hold of my person it is more dear than my estate.

Thomas Rainborough: I do very well remember that the gentleman in the window[13] said that, if it were so, there were no propriety to be had, because five parts of the nation, the poor people, are now excluded and would then come in. So one on the other side said that, if it were otherwise, then rich men only shall be chosen. Then, I say, the one part shall make hewers of wood and drawers of water of the other five, and so the greatest part of the nation be enslaved. Truly I think we are still where we were; and I do not hear any argument given but only that it is the present law of the kingdom. I say still, what shall become of those many men that have laid out themselves for the Parliament of England in this present war, that have ruined themselves by fighting, by hazarding all they had? They are Englishmen. They have now nothing to say for themselves.

Rich: I should be very sorry to speak anything here that should give offence, or that may occasion personal reflections that we spoke against just now.[14] I did not urge anything so far as was represented, and I did not at all urge that there should be a consideration had of rich men, and that a man that is poor shall be without consideration, or that he deserves to be made poorer and not to live in independence at all. But all that I urged was this: that I think it worthy consideration, whether they should have an equality in their interest. However, I think we have been a great while upon this point, and if we be as long upon all the rest, it were well if there were no greater difference than this.

Hugh Peter:[15] I think that this matter of the franchise may be easily agreed on, that is, there may be a way thought of. I think you would do well to sit up all night if thereby you could effect it, but I think that three or four might be thought of in this company to form a committee. You will be forced only to put characters upon electors or elected; therefore I do suppose that if there be any here that can make up a representative to your mind, the thing is gained. But I would fain know whether that will answer the work of your meeting. The question is, whether you can state any one question for removing the present danger of the kingdom, whether any one question or no will dispatch the work.

Sir, I desire, if it be possible, that some question may be stated to finish the present work, to cement us in the points wherein lies the distance; and if the thoughts be of the commonwealth and the people's freedom, I think that's soon cured. I desire that all manner of plainness may be used, that we may not go on with the lapwing and carry one another off the nest. There is something else that must cement us where the awkwardness of our spirits lies.

Thomas Rainborough: For my part, I think we cannot engage one way or other in the army if we do not think of the people's liberties. If we can agree where the liberty and freedom of the people lies, that will do all.

Ireton: I cannot consent so far. As I said before, when I see the hand of God destroying king, and Lords, and Commons too, or any foundation of human constitution, when I see God has done it, I shall, I hope, comfortably acquiesce in it. But first, I cannot give my consent to it, because it is not good. And secondly, as I desire that this army should have regard to engagements wherever they are lawful, so I would have them have regard to this as well: that they should not bring that scandal upon the name of God and the Saints, that those that call themselves by that name, those whom God has owned and appeared with, that we should represent ourselves to the world as men so far from being of that peaceable spirit which is suitable to the Gospel, as we should have bought peace of the world upon such terms – as we would not have peace in the world but upon such terms – as should destroy all property. If the principle upon which you move this alteration, or the ground upon which you press that we should make this alteration, do destroy all kind of property or whatsoever a man has by human constitution, I cannot consent to it. The law of God does not give me property, nor the law of nature, but property is of human constitution. I have a property and this I shall enjoy. Constitution founds property. If either the thing itself that you press or the consequence of that you press do destroy property, though I shall acquiesce in having no property, yet I cannot give my heart or hand to it; because it is a thing evil in itself and scandalous to the world, and I desire this army may be free from both.

Sexby: I see that though liberty were our end, there is a degeneration from it. We have engaged in this kingdom and ventured our lives, and it was all for this: to recover our birthrights and privileges as Englishmen; and by the arguments urged there is none. There are many thousands of us soldiers that have ventured our lives; we have had little propriety in the kingdom as to our estates, yet we have had a birthright. But it seems now, except a man has a fixed estate in this kingdom, he has no right in this kingdom. I wonder we were so much deceived. If we had not a right to the kingdom, we were mere mercenary soldiers. There are many in my condition, that have as good a condition as I have; it may be little estate they have at present, and yet they have as much a birthright as those too who are their lawgivers, as any in this place. I shall tell you in a word my resolution. I am resolved to give my birthright to none. Whatsoever may come in the way, and whatsoever may be thought, I will give it to none. If this thing be denied the poor, that with so much pressing after they have sought, it will be the greatest scandal. There was one thing spoken to this effect: that if the poor and those in low condition were given their birthright it would be the destruction of this kingdom. I think this was but a distrust of providence. I do think the poor and meaner of this kingdom – I speak as in relation to the condition of soldiers, in which we are – have been the means of the preservation of this kingdom. I say, in their stations, and really I think to their utmost possibility; and their lives have not been held dear for purchasing the good of the kingdom. And now they demand the birthright for which they fought. Those that act to this end are as free from anarchy or confusion as those that oppose it, and they have the law of God and the law of their conscience with them. But truly I shall only sum up in this: I desire that we may not spend so much time upon these things. We must be plain. When men come to understand these things, they will not lose that which they have contended for. That which I shall beseech you is to come to a determination of this question.

Ireton: I am very sorry we are come to this point, that from reasoning one to another we should come to express our resolutions. I profess for my part, what I see is good for the kingdom, and becoming a Christian to contend for, I hope through God I shall have strength and resolution to do my part towards it. And yet I will profess direct contrary in some kind to what that gentleman said. For my part, rather than I will make a disturbance to a good constitution of a kingdom wherein I may live in godliness and honesty, and peace and quietness, I will part with a great deal of my birthright. I will part with my own property rather than I will be the man that shall make a disturbance in the kingdom for my property; and therefore if all the people in this kingdom, or the representatives of them all together, should meet and should give away my property I would submit to it, I would give it away. But that gentleman, and I think every Christian, ought to bear that spirit, to carry that in him, that he will not make a public disturbance upon a private prejudice.

Now let us consider where our difference lies. We all agree that you should have a representative to govern, and this representative to be as equal as you can make it. But the question is, whether this distribution can be made to all persons equally, or whether only amongst those equals that have the interest of England in them? That which I have declared is my opinion still. I think we ought to keep to that constitution which we have now, both because it is a civil constitution (it is the most fundamental constitution that we have) and because there is so much justice and reason and prudence in it – as I dare confidently undertake to demonstrate – that there are many more evils that will follow in case you do alter it than there can be in the standing of it. But I say but this in the general: that I do wish that they that talk of birthrights – we any of us when we talk of birthrights – would consider what really our birthright is. If a man mean by birthright, whatsoever I can challenge by the law of nature (suppose there were no constitution at all, no civil law and no civil constitution), and that that I am to contend for against constitution, then you leave no property, nor no foundation for any man to enjoy anything. But if you call that your birthright which is the most fundamental part of your constitution, then let him perish that goes about to hinder you or any man of the least part of your birthright, or will desire to do it. But if you will lay aside the most fundamental constitution (which is as good, for all you can discern, as anything you can propose) at least it is a constitution, and I will give you consequence for consequence of good upon that constitution as you can give upon your birthright without it; and if you merely upon pretence of a birthright – of the right of nature, which is only true as for your being, and not for your better being – if you will upon that ground pretend that this constitution, the most fundamental constitution, the thing that has reason and equity in it, shall not stand in your way, it is the same principle to me, say I, as if but for your better satisfaction you shall take hold of anything that another man calls his own.

Thomas Rainborough: Sir, I see that it is impossible to have liberty but all property must be taken away. If it be laid down for a rule, and if you will say it, it must be so. But I would fain know what the soldier has fought for all this while? He has fought to enslave himself, to give power to men of riches, men of estates, to make him a perpetual slave. We do find in all presses that go forth none must be pressed that are freehold men. When these gentlemen fall out among themselves they shall press the poor scrubs to come and kill one another for them.[16]

Ireton: I confess I see so much right in the business that I am not easily satisfied with flourishes. If you will not lay the stress of the business upon the consideration of reason, or right relating to anything of human constitution, or anything of that nature, but will put it upon consequences, I will show you greater ill consequences; I see enough to say that, to my apprehensions, I can show you greater ill consequences to follow upon that alteration which you would have, by extending voices to all that have a being in this kingdom, than any that can come by this present constitution, a great deal. That that you urge of the present constitution is a particular ill consequence. This that I object against your proposal is a general ill consequence, and this is as great as that or any ill consequence else whatsoever, though I think you will see that the validity of that argument must be that for one ill that lies upon that which now is, I can show you a thousand upon this that you propose.

Give me leave to say but this one word. I will tell you what the soldier of the kingdom has fought for. First, the danger that we stood in was that one man's will must be a law. The people of the kingdom must have this right at least, that they should not be concluded but by the representative of those that had the interest of the kingdom. Some men fought in this, because they were immediately concerned and engaged in it; other men who had no other interest in the kingdom but this, that they should have the benefit of those laws made by the representative, yet fought that they should have the benefit of this representative. They thought it was better to be concluded by the common consent of those that were fixed men, and settled men, that had the interest of this kingdom in them. 'And from that way,' said they, 'I shall know a law and have a certainty.' Every man that was born in the country, that is a denizen[17] in it, that has a freedom, he was capable of trading to get money, to get estates by; and therefore this man, I think, had a great deal of reason to build up such a foundation of interest to himself; that is, that the will of one man should not be a law, but that the law of this kingdom should be by a choice of persons to represent, and that choice to be made by, the generality of the kingdom. Here was a right that induced men to fight, and those men that had this interest, though this be not the utmost interest that other men have, yet they had some interest.

Now tell me why we should go to plead whatsoever we can challenge by the right of nature against whatsoever any man can challenge by constitution. I do not see where that man will stop, as to point of property, so that he shall not use against other property that right he has claimed by the law of nature against that constitution. I desire any man to show me where there is a difference. I have been answered, 'Now we see liberty cannot stand without destroying property.' Liberty may be had and property not be destroyed. First, the liberty of all those that have the permanent interest in the kingdom, that is provided for by the constitution. And secondly, by an appeal to the law of nature liberty cannot be provided for in a general sense, if property be preserved. For if property be preserved by acknowledging a natural right in the possessor, so that I am not to meddle with such a man's estate, his meat, his drink, his apparel, or other goods, then the right of nature destroys liberty. By the right of nature I am to have sustenance rather than perish; yet property destroys it for a man to have this by the right of nature, even suppose there be no human constitution.

Peter: I do say still, under favour, there is a way to cure all this debate. I will mind you of one thing: that upon the will of one man abusing us, we reached agreement, and if the safety of the army be in danger so we may again. I hope, it is not denied by any man that any wise, discreet man that has preserved England is worthy of a voice in the government of it. So that, I profess to you, for my part I am clear the point of election should be amended in that sense. I think, they will desire no more liberty. If there were time to dispute it, I think they would be satisfied, and all will be satisfied.

Cromwell: I confess I was most dissatisfied with that I heard Mr Sexby speak, of any man here, because it did savour so much of will. But I desire that all of us may decline that, and if we meet here really to agree to that which is for the safety of the kingdom, let us not spend so much time in such debates as these are, but let us apply ourselves to such things as are conclusive, and that shall be this. Everybody here would be willing that the representative might be mended, that is, that it might be made better than it is. Perhaps it may be offered in 'The heads of the proposals' too lamely. If the thing there insisted upon be too limited, why perhaps there are a very considerable part of copyholders by inheritance that ought to have a voice; and there may be somewhat in that paper too that reflects upon the generality of the people in denying them a voice. I know our debates are endless if we think to bring it to an issue this way. If we may but resolve upon a committee, things may be done. If I cannot be satisfied to go so far as these gentlemen that bring the 'Agreement', I say it again and I profess it, I shall freely and willingly withdraw myself, and I hope to do it in such a manner that the army shall see that I shall by my withdrawing satisfy the interest of the army, the public interest of the kingdom, and those ends these men aim at. And I think if you do bring this to a result it were well.

Thomas Rainborough: If these men must be advanced, and other men set under foot, I am not satisfied. If their rules must be observed, and other men, that are not in authority, be silenced, I do not know how this can stand together with the idea of a free debate. I wonder how that should be thought wilfulness in one man that is reason in another; for I confess I have not heard anything that does satisfy me, and though I have not so much wisdom, or so many notions in my head, I have so many apprehensions that I could tell a hundred such of the ruin of the people. I am not at all against a committee's meeting; and as you say – and I think every Christian ought to do the same – for my part I shall be ready, if I see the way that I am going, and the thing that I would insist on, will destroy the kingdom, I shall withdraw from it as soon as any. And therefore, till I see that, I shall use all the means I can, and I think it is no fault in any man to refuse to sell that which is his birthright.

Sexby: I desire to speak a few words. I am sorry that my zeal to what I apprehend is good should be so ill resented. I am not sorry to see that which I apprehend is truth disputed, but I am sorry the Lord has darkened some so much as not to see it, and that is in short this. Do you not think it were a sad and miserable condition, that we have fought all this time for nothing? All here, both great and small, do think that we fought for something. I confess, many of us fought for those ends which, we since saw, were not those which caused us to go through difficulties and straits and to venture all in the ship with you; it had been good in you to have advertised us of it, and I believe you would have had fewer under your command to have commanded. But if this be the business, that an estate does make men capable – it is no matter which way they get it, they are capable – to choose those that shall represent them, I think there are many that have not estates that in honesty have as much right in the freedom of their choice as any that have great estates. Truly, sir, as for your putting off this question and coming to some other, I dare say, and I dare appeal to all of them, that they cannot settle upon any other until this be done. It was the ground that we took up arms on, and it is the ground which we shall maintain. Concerning my making rents and divisions in this way: as a particular individual, if I were but so, I could lie down and be trodden there; but truly I am sent by a regiment, and if I should not speak, guilt shall lie upon me, and I should think I were a covenant-breaker. I do not know how we have been answered in our arguments, and as for our engagements, I conceive we shall not accomplish them to the kingdom when we deny them to ourselves. I shall be loath to make a rent and division, but, for my own part, unless I see this put to a question, I despair of an issue. [. . .]

Ireton: I should not speak again, but reflections do necessitate it, do call upon us to vindicate ourselves. As if we, who have led men into engagements and services, had divided from them because we did not concur with them! I will ask that gentleman that spoke (whom I love in my heart): whether when they drew out to serve the Parliament in the beginning, whether then they engaged with the army at New-market, whether then they thought of any more interest or right in the kingdom than this; whether they did think that they should have as great interest in Parliament-men as freeholders had, or whether from the beginning we did not engage for the liberty of Parliaments, and that we should be concluded by the laws that such did make. Unless somebody did make you believe before now that you should have an equal interest in the kingdom, unless somebody did make that to be believed, there is no reason to blame men for leading you so far as they have done; and if any man was far enough from such an apprehension, that man has not been deceived.

And truly, I shall say but this word more for myself in this business, because the whole objection seems to be pressed to me, and main-tained against me. I will not arrogate that I was the first man that put the army upon the thought either of successive Parliaments or more equal Parliaments; yet there are some here that know who they were that put us upon that foundation of liberty of putting a period to this Parliament, in order that we might have successive Parliaments, and that there might be a more equal distribution of elections. There are many here that know who were the first movers of that business in the army. I shall not arrogate that to myself, but I can argue this with a clear conscience: that no man has prosecuted that with more earn-estness, and will stand to that interest more than I do, of having Parliaments successive and not perpetual, and the distribution of elections more equal. But, notwithstanding, my opinion stands good, that it ought to be a distribution amongst the fixed and settled people of this nation; it's more prudent and safe, and more upon this ground of right for it to be so. Now it is the fundamental constitution of this kingdom; and that which you take away you take away for matter of wilfulness. Notwithstanding, as for this universal conclusion, that all inhabitants shall have voices, as it stands in the 'Agreement', I must declare that though I cannot yet be satisfied, yet for my part I shall acquiesce; I will not make a distraction in this army. Though I have a property in being one of those that should be an elector, though I have an interest in the birthright, yet I will rather lose that birthright and that interest than I will make it my business to oppose them, if I see but the generality of those whom I have reason to think honest men and conscientious men and godly men, to carry themselves another way. I will not oppose, though I be not satisfied to join with them. And I desire to say this: I am agreed with you if you insist upon a more equal distribution of elections; I will agree with you, not only to dispute for it, but to fight for it and contend for it. Thus far I shall agree with you. On the other hand, to those who differ in their terms and say, 'I will not agree with you except you go farther,' I make answer, 'Thus far I can go with you: I will go with you as far as I can.' If you will appoint a committee of some few to consider of that, so as you preserve the equitable part of that constitution that now is, securing a voice to those who are like to be freemen, men not given up to the wills of others, and thereby keeping to the latitude which is the equity of constitutions, I will go with you as far as I can. And where I cannot I will sit down, I will not make any disturbance among you.

Thomas Rainborough: If I do speak my soul and conscience I do think that there is not an objection made but that it has been answered; but the speeches are so long. I am sorry for some passion and some reflections, and I could wish where it is most taken amiss the cause had not been given. It is a fundamental of the constitution of the kingdom, that there be Parliamentary boroughs; I would fain know whether the choice of burgesses in corporations should not be altered.

But the end wherefore I speak is only this: you think we shall be worse than we are, if we come to a conclusion by a sudden vote. If it be put to the question we shall at least all know one another's mind. If it be determined, and the common resolutions known, we shall take such a course as to put it in execution. This gentleman says, if he cannot go he will sit still. He thinks he has a full liberty to do so; we think we have not. There is a great deal of difference between us two. If a man has all he does desire, he may wish to sit still; but if I think I have nothing at all of what I fought for, I do not think the argument holds that I must desist as well as he.

Petty: The rich would very unwillingly be concluded by the poor. And there is as much reason that the rich should conclude the poor as the poor the rich – and indeed that is no reason at all. There should be an equal share in both. I understood your engagement was that you would use all your endeavours for the liberties of the people, that they should be secured. If there is such a constitution that the people are not free, that constitution should be annulled. That constitution which is now set up is a constitution of forty shillings a year, but this constitution does not make the people free.

Cromwell: Here's the mistake: you make the whole question to be whether that's the better constitution in that paper, or that which now is. But if you will go upon such a ground as that, although a better constitution was really offered for the removing of the worse, yet some gentlemen are resolved to stick to the worse and there might be a great deal of prejudice upon such an apprehension. I think you are by this time satisfied that it is a clear mistake; for it is a dispute whether or no this proposed constitution be better, whether it be not destructive to the kingdom. [. . .]

Captain John Clarke:[18] I presume that the great stick here is this: that if everyone shall have his natural propriety of election it does bereave the kingdom of its principal fundamental constitution, that it now has. I presume that all people, and all nations whatsoever, have a liberty and power to alter and change their constitutions if they find them to be weak and infirm. Now if the people of England shall find this weakness in their constitution, they may change it if they please. Another thing is this: it is feared that if the light of nature be only followed in this, it may destroy the propriety which every man can call his own. But it will not, and the reason is this, because this principle and light of nature does give all men their own – as, for example, the clothes upon my back because they are not another man's. Finally, if every man has this propriety of election to choose those who shall make the laws, you fear it may beget inconveniencies. I do not conceive that anything may be so nicely and precisely done but that it may admit of inconveniency. If it be that there is inconveniency in that form of the constitution wherein it is now, there may some of those inconveniencies rise from the changes, that are apprehended from them. For my part I know nothing of fatal consequence in the relation of men but the want of love in it, and then, if difference arises, the sword must decide it.

I too shall desire that before the question be stated it may be moderated as for foreigners. [. . .]

Ireton: I have declared that you will alter that constitution from a better to a worse, from a just to a thing that is less just in my apprehension; and I will not repeat the reasons of that, but refer to what I have declared before. To me, if there were nothing but this, that there is a constitution, and that constitution which is the very last constitution, which if you take away you leave nothing of constitution, and consequently nothing of right or property, it would be enough. I would not go to alter this, though a man could propound that which in some respects might be better, unless it could be demonstrated to me that this were unlawful, or that this were destructive. Truly, therefore, I say for my part, to go on a sudden to make such a limitation as that to inhabitants in general, is to make no limitation at all. If you do extend the latitude of the constitution so far that any man shall have a voice in election who has not that interest in this kingdom that is permanent and fixed, who has not that interest upon which he may have his freedom in this kingdom without dependence, you will put it into the hands of men to choose, not of men desirous to preserve their liberty, but of men who will give it away.

I am confident, our discontent and dissatisfaction if ever they do well, they do in this. If there be anything at all that is a foundation of liberty it is this, that those who shall choose the lawmakers shall be men freed from dependence upon others. I have a thing put into my heart which I cannot but speak. I profess I am afraid that if we, from such apprehensions as these are of an imaginable right of nature opposite to constitution, if we will contend and hazard the breaking of peace upon this business of that enlargement, I think if we, from imaginations and conceits, will go about to hazard the peace of the kingdom, to alter the constitution in such a point, I am afraid we shall find the hand of God will follow it and we shall see that that liberty which we so much talk of, and have so much contended for, shall be nothing at all by this our contending for it, by our putting it into the hands of those men that will give it away when they have it.

Cromwell: If we should go about to alter these things, I do not think that we are bound to fight for every particular proposition. Servants, while servants, are not included. Then you agree that he that receives alms is to be excluded?

Lieutenant-Colonel Thomas Read:[19] I suppose it's concluded by all, that the choosing of representatives is a privilege; now I see no reason why any man that is a native ought to be excluded that privilege, unless from voluntary servitude.

Petty: I conceive the reason why we would exclude apprentices, or servants, or those that take alms, is because they depend upon the will of other men and should be afraid to displease them. For servants and apprentices, they are included in their masters, and so for those that receive alms from door to door; but if there be any general way taken for those that are not so bound to the will of other men, it would be well. [. . .]

Thomas Rainborough moved: That the army might be called to a rendezvous, and things settled as promised in its printed engagements.

Ireton: We are called back to engagements. I think the engagements we have made and published, and all the engagements of all sorts, have been better kept by those that did not so much cry out for it than by those that do, and – if you will have it in plain terms – better kept than by those that have brought this paper. Give me leave to tell you, in that one point, in the engagement of the army not to divide, I am sure that he that understands the engagement of the army not to divide or disband as meaning that we are not to divide for quarters, for the ease of the country, or the satisfaction of service, he that does understand it in that sense, I am not capable of his understanding. There was another sense in it, and that is, that we should not suffer ourselves to be torn into pieces. Such a dividing as that is really a disbanding, and for my part I do not know what disbanding is if not that dividing. I say that the subscribers of this paper, the authors of that book that is called 'The case of the army', I say that they have gone the way of disbanding. Disbanding of an army is not parting in a place, for if that be so, did we not at that night disband to several quarters? Did we not then send several regiments: Colonel Scroope's regiment into the West, we know where it was first; Colonel Horton's regiment into Wales for preventing of insurrection there; Colonel Lambert's and Colonel Lilburne's regiments then sent down for strengthening such a place as York? And yet the authors of that paper and the subscribers of it – for I cannot think the authors and subscribers all one – know, and well they may know it, that there is not one part of the army is divided in body farther than the outcries of the authors of it are in spirit.[. . .]

An unnamed agitator. Whereas you say the agents did it, it was the soldiers did put the agents upon these meetings. It was the dissatisfactions that were in the army which provoked, which occasioned, those meetings, which you suppose tends so much to dividing; and the reasons of such dissatisfactions are because those whom they had to trust to act for them were not true to them.

If this be all the effect of your meetings to agree upon the 'Agreement', there is but one thing in this that has not been insisted upon and propounded by the army heretofore, in 'The heads of the proposals', and all along. Here the franchise is put according to the number of inhabitants; there according to the taxes. This says a period to be put to the Parliament at such a day, the last of September; the other says a period within a year at most. The 'Agreement' says that the representers have the power of making law, and determining what is law, without the consent of another. 'Tis true the 'Proposals' said not that but would restore the consent of the king. And for my part, if any man will put that to the question whether we shall concur with it, I am in the same mind still, especially if by your franchise you put it in any other hands than of those that are freemen. But even if you shall put the question with that limitation to freemen that have been all along acknowledged by the Parliament, till we can acquit ourselves justly from any engagement (old or new) that we stand in, to preserve the person of the king, the persons of lords, and their rights, so far as they are consistent with the common right and the safety of the kingdom, till that be done, I think there is reason that that exception in their favour should continue, but with the proviso which has been all along – that is, where the safety of the kingdom is concerned. This the 'Proposals' seem to hold out.

I would hold to positive constitution where I see things would not do real mischief. I would neither be thought to be a wrong-doer or disturber; so long as I can with safety continue a constitution I will do it. And therefore where I find that the safety of the kingdom is not concerned, I would not for every trifling cause make that this shall be a law, though neither the Lords, who have a claim to it, nor the king, who has a claim to it, will consent. But where this safety is concerned I think that particular rights cannot stand. Upon the whole matter let men but consider whether those that have thus gone away to divide from the army will not destroy the constitution upon a fancied right and advantage of the people. Admit that this 'Agreement of the people' be the advantage, it may be. Shall we then agree to that without any limitation?

I do agree that the king is bound by his oath at his coronation to agree to the law that the Commons shall choose without Lords or anybody else. But if I can agree any further, that if the king do not confirm with his authority the laws that the people shall choose those laws require not his authority, we know what will follow.

Petty: I had the happiness sometimes to be at the debate of the 'Proposals', and my opinion was then as it is now, against the king's vote and the Lords'. But I did not then so definitely desire the abolition of these votes as I do now desire it; for since that time it has pleased God to raise a company of men that do stand up for the power of the House of Commons, which is the representative of the people, and deny the negative voice of king and Lords. For my part I was much unknown to any of them, but I heard their principles; and hearing their principles I cannot but join with them in my judgement, for I think it is reasonable that all laws are made by the people's consent alone. Whereas you seem to make the king and Lords so light a thing as that it may be without prejudice to keep them, though to the destruction of the kingdom to throw them out; for my part I cannot but think that both the power of king and Lords was ever a branch of tyranny. And if ever a people shall free themselves from tyranny, certainly it is after seven years' war and fighting for their liberty. For my part I think that if the constitution of this kingdom shall be established as formerly, it might rivet tyranny into this kingdom more strongly than before. For when the people shall hear that for seven years together the people were plundered, and that after they had overcome the king and kept the king under restraint, at last the king comes in again, then it will rivet the king's interest; and so when any men shall endeavour to free themselves from tyranny we may do them mischief and no good. I think it's most just and equal, since a number of men have declared against it, that they should be encouraged in it, and not discouraged. And I find by the council that their thoughts are the same against the king and Lords, and if so be that a power may be raised to do that, it would do well.

Wildman: Truly, sir, I being desired by the agents yesterday to appear at council or committees either, at that time in their behalf, I suppose I may be bold to make known what I know of their sense, and a little to vindicate them in their way of proceeding, and to show the necessity of this way of proceeding that they have entered upon.

Truly, sir, as to breaking of engagements, the agents do declare their principle, that whenever any engagement cannot be kept justly they must break that engagement. Now though it's urged they ought to condescend to what the General Council do resolve, I conceive it's true only so long as it is for their safety. I conceive it's just and righteous for them to stand up for some more speedy vigorous actings. I conceive it's no more than what the army did when the Parliament did not only delay deliverance, but opposed it. And I conceive this way of their appearing has not been in the least way anything tending to division, since they proceed to clear the rights of the people; and so long as they proceed upon those righteous principles for which we first engaged, I suppose it cannot be laid to their charge that they are dividers. And though it be declared that they ought to stand only as soldiers and not as Englishmen, yet the malice of the enemies would have bereaved you of your liberties as Englishmen, and therefore as Englishmen they are deeply concerned to regard the due observation of their rights, and have the same right to declare their apprehensions as I, or any commoner, have right to propound to the kingdom my conceptions of what is fit for the good of the kingdom.

Whereas it is objected, 'How will it appear that their proceedings shall tend for the good of the kingdom?', that matter is different from the point of justice they would propound. Whereas it was said before, it was propounded in the council, that there must be an end to the present Parliament and an equality as to elections, I find it to be their minds also; but when they came there, they found many aversions from matters that they ought to stand to as soldiers and as Englishmen, and therefore, I find, it was discovered that there was a difference concerning the matter of the thing, and I conceive it to be a very vast difference in the whole matter of the 'Proposals'. By it the foundation of slavery was riveted more strongly than before, as where the militia is instated in the king and Lords, and not in the Commons, and there too is a foundation of a future quarrel constantly laid. However, the main thing was that the right of the militia was acknowledged to be in the king, as they found in the 'Proposals' propounded, before any redress of any one of the people's grievances or any one of their burdens; and the king was so to be brought in as with a negative voice, whereby the people and army that have fought against him when he had propounded such things, would be at his mercy. And finding this, they perceived they were, as they thought, in a sad case; for they thought, he coming in thus with a negative voice, the Parliament are but as so many ciphers, so many round O's, for if the king would not do it, he might choose, *Sic volo, sic jubeo*, etc.,[20] and so the corrupt party of the kingdom must be so settled in the king. The godly people are turned over and trampled upon already in the most places of the kingdom. I speak but the words of the agents, and I find this to be their thoughts.

But whereas it is said, 'How will this 'Agreement' provide for anything for that purpose?', I shall say that this paper does lay down the foundations of freedom for all manner of people. It does lay the foundations of soldiers' freedom, whereas they found a great uncertainty in the 'Proposals', which implied that they should go to the king for an Act of Indemnity, and thus the king might command his judges to hang them up for what they did in the wars, because, the present constitution being left as it was, nothing was law but what the king signed, and not any ordinance of Parliament without his consent. And considering this, they thought it should be by an agreement with the people, whereby a rule between the Parliament and the people might be set, that so they might be destroyed neither by the king's prerogative nor Parliament's privileges (including those of the Lords, for they are not bound to be subject to the laws as other men, and that is why men cannot recover their estates). They thought there must be a necessity of a rule between the Parliament and the people, so that the Parliament should know what they were entrusted with, and what they were not; and that there might be no doubt of the Parliament's power, to lay foundations of future quarrels. The Parliament shall not meddle with a soldier after indemnity if it is so agreed amongst the people; whereas between a Parliament and a king the soldier may lose his indemnity. If the king were not under restraint his assent might be made to bind him. But if the present Parliament should make an Act of Indemnity, who shall say that another Parliament cannot alter this? 'An agreement of the people' would be necessary, that these foundations might be established, that there might be no dispute between Lords and Commons, and that, these things being settled, there should be no more disputes at all, but that the Parliament should redress the people's grievances. Whereas now almost all are troubled with the king's interests, if this were settled the Parliament should be free from these temptations. And besides – which for my own part I do suppose to be a truth – this very Parliament, by the king's voice in this very Parliament, may destroy us, whereas then they shall be free from temptations and the king cannot have an influence upon them such as he now has. [. . .]

At the General Council of the Army at Putney, 1st November 1647.

[*The record of the discussions on 29 October comes to an abrupt and inconclusive end. However, on the third recorded day of the debates, the proceedings in Putney church returned to the issue of the position of the king and the Lords in any future settlement.*]

[. . .] *William Allen*:[21] My desire is to see things put to an issue. Men have been declaring their thoughts, and truly I would crave liberty to declare mine. The difference between us, I think, is in the interest of king and Lords, some declaring against the name and title of king and Lords, others preferring to retain them. For my part I think, clearly, according to what we have engaged we stand bound; and I think we should be looked upon as persons not fit to be called Christians, if we do not work up to them. As first, concerning the king: you say you will set up the king as far as may be consistent with, and not prejudicial to, the liberties of the kingdom; and really I am of that mind too. If the setting up of him be not consistent with them, and prejudicial to them, then down with him; but if he may be so set up – which I think he may – then set him up, and it is not our judgement only, but of all save those that set forth 'The case of the army'.

Thomas Rainborough took occasion to take notice as if what Mr Allen spoke did reflect upon himself or some other there, as if it were asserted that they were against the name of king and Lords.

Sexby: Truly I must be bold to offer this one word unto you. Here was somewhat before spoke of the workings and actings of God within us; I shall speak a word of that. The Lord has put you into a state, or at least suffered you to run yourselves into such a one, that you know not where you are. You are in a wilderness condition. Some actings among us singly and jointly are the cause of it. Truly I would entreat you to weigh that. We find in the word of God, 'I would heal Babylon, but she would not be healed.' I think that we have gone about to heal Babylon when she would not. We have gone about to wash a blackamoor, to wash him white, which he will not. We are going about to set up that power which God will destroy: I think we are going about to set up the power of kings, some part of it, which God will destroy; and which will be but as a burdensome stone that whosoever shall fall upon it, it will destroy him. I think this is the reason of the straits that are in hand. I shall propose this to your Honours, to weigh the grounds, whether they be right, and then you shall be led in pleasant paths by still waters, and shall not be offended.

Cromwell: [. . .] Truly we have heard many speaking to us; and I cannot but think that in many of those things God has spoke to us. I cannot but think that in most that have spoke there has been something of God laid forth to us; and yet there have been several contradictions in what has been spoken. But certainly God is not the author of contradictions. The contradictions are not so much in the end as in the way. I cannot see but that we all speak to the same end, and the mistakes are only in the way. The end is to deliver this nation from oppression and slavery, to accomplish that work that God has carried us on in, to establish our hopes of an end of justice and righteousness in it. We agree thus far. Further too: that we all apprehend danger from the person of the king and from the Lords; I think we may go thus far farther, that all that have spoke have agreed in this too, though the gentleman in the window[22] seemed to deny it when he spoke of setting up, but he, if he would declare it, did not mean all that that word might import. I think that seems to be general among us all, that there is not any intention of any in the army, of any of us, to set up the one or the other. If it were free before us whether we should set up one or the other, I do to my best observation find an unanimity amongst us all, that we would set up neither. Thus far I find us to be agreed; and thus far as we are agreed, I think it is of God. But there are circumstances in which we differ as in relation to this. Then I must further tell you that as we do not make it our business or intention to set up the one or the other, so neither is it our intention to preserve the one or the other, with a visible danger and destruction to the people and the public interest. So that that part of difference that seems to be among us is whether there can be a preservation of them with safety to the kingdom. First of all, on the one part, there is this apprehension: that we cannot with justice and righteousness at the present destroy, or go about to destroy, or take away, or altogether lay aside, both, or all the interest they have in the public affairs of the kingdom; and those that do so apprehend would strain something in point of security, would rather leave some hazard, or at least, if they see that they may consist without any considerable hazard to the interest of the kingdom, do so far wish to preserve them. On the other hand, those who differ from this, I do take it (in the most candid apprehension) that they seem to run thus: that there is not any safety or security to the liberty of the kingdom, and to the public interest, if you do retain these at all; and therefore they think this is a consideration to them paramount to the consideration of particular obligations of justice, or matter of right or due towards king or Lords. [. . .]

As to the dispensations of God, it was more particular in the time of the law of Moses than in the time of the law written in our hearts, that word within us, the mind of Christ; and truly when we have no other more particular impression of the power of God going forth with us, I think that this law and this word speaking within us, which truly is in every man who has the spirit of God, we are to have a regard to. [. . .] For my part I do not know any outward evidence of what proceeds from the spirit of God more clear than this, the appearance of meekness and gentleness and mercy and patience and forbearance and love, and a desire to do good to all, and to destroy none than can be saved. And for my part I say, where I do see this, where I do see men speaking according to this law which I am sure is the law of the spirit of life I am satisfied. But I cannot but take that to be contrary to this law, which is, of the spirit of malice and envy, and things of that nature. And I think there is this radically in that heart where there is such a law as leads us against all opposition. On the other hand, I think that he that would decline the doing of justice where there is no place for mercy, and the exercise of the ways of force, for the safety of the kingdom, where there is no other way to save it, and would decline these out of the apprehensions of danger and difficulties in it, he that leads that way, on the other hand, does also truly lead us from that which is the law of the spirit of life, the law written in our hearts.

[. . .] I could wish that none of those whose apprehensions run that there can be no safety in a consistency with the person of the king or the Lords, or in their having the least interest in the public affairs of the kingdom, I do wish that they will take heed of that which some men are apt to be carried away by, namely apprehensions that God will destroy these persons or that power; for that they may mistake in. And though I myself do concur with them, and perhaps concur with them upon some ground that God will do so, yet let us not make those things to be our rule which we cannot so clearly know to be the mind of God. I mean in particular things let us not make those our rules: that 'this is to be done; this is the mind of God; we must work to it.' But at least let those to whom this is not made clear, though they do think it probable that God will destroy them, yet let them make this a rule to themselves: 'Though God have a purpose to destroy them, and though I should find a desire to destroy them – though a Christian spirit can hardly find it for itself – yet

God can do it without necessitating us to do a thing which is scandalous, or sin, or which would bring a dishonour to his name.' And therefore those that are of that mind, let them wait upon God for such a way when the thing may be done without sin, and without scandal too. [. . .]

Captain George Bishop:[23] I shall desire to speak one word, and that briefly. After many inquiries in my spirit what's the reason that we are distracted in counsel, and that we cannot, as formerly, preserve the kingdom from that dying condition in which it is, I find this answer, the answer which is vouchsafed to many Christians besides, amongst us. I say it not in respect of any particular persons, but I say that the reason is a compliance to preserve that man of blood,[24] and those principles of tyranny, which God from heaven by his many successes given has manifestly declared against, and which, I am confident, may yet be our destruction if they be preserved. I only speak this as what is upon my spirit, because I see you are upon inquiry what God has given in to anyone, which may tend to the preservation of the kingdom.

Wildman: I observe that the work has been to inquire what has been the mind of God, and every one speaks what is given in to his spirit. I desire as much as is possible to reverence whatsoever has the spirit or image of God upon it. Whatever another man has received from the spirit, that man cannot demonstrate it to me but by some other way than merely relating to me that which he conceives to be the mind of God. In spiritual matters he must show its conformity with scripture, though indeed it is beyond the power of the reason of all the men on earth to demonstrate the scriptures to be the scriptures written by the spirit of God, and it must be the spirit of faith in a man himself that must finally make him believe whatsoever may be spoken in spiritual matters. The case is yet more difficult in civil matters; for we cannot find anything in the word of God of what is fit to be done in civil matters. But I conceive that only is of God that does appear to be like unto God – to practise justice and mercy, to be meek and peaceable. I should desire therefore that we might proceed only in that way, if it please this honourable council, to consider what is justice and what is mercy, and what is good, and I cannot but conclude that that is of God. Otherwise I cannot think that any one does speak from God when he says what he speaks is of God.

But to the matter in hand. I am clearly of opinion with that gentleman that spoke last save one,[25] that it is not of God to decline the doing of justice where there is no way left of mercy; and I could much concur that it is very questionable whether there be a way left for mercy upon that person that we now insist upon. I would know whether it is demonstrable by reason or justice, that it is right to punish with death those that according to his command do make war, or those that do but hold compliance with them, and then to say that there is a way left for mercy for him who was the great actor of this, and who was the great contriver of all? But I confess because it is in civil matters I would much decline that, and rather look to what is safety, what the mind does dictate from safety. What is for the safety of the people, I know it cannot be the mind of God to go contrary to that. But for what particulars that gentleman speaks, of the differences between us, I think they are so many as not easily to be reckoned up. That which he instanced was that some did desire to preserve the person of the king and persons of the Lords, so far as it was consistent with the safety or the good of the kingdom, and other persons do conceive that the preservation of the king or Lords was inconsistent with the people's safety, and that law to be paramount to all considerations.

Ireton: Sir, I think he did not speak of the destroying of the king and Lords – I have not heard any man charge all the Lords so as to deserve a punishment – but of a reserving to them any interest at all in the public affairs of the kingdom.

Wildman, addressing Cromwell: Then, sir, as I conceive, you were saying the difference was this: that some persons were of opinion that they stood engaged to the preservation of the power of king and Lords, while others held that the safety of the people was paramount to all considerations, and might keep them from any giving them what was their due and right.

Ireton: I think it was said that while some men did apprehend that there might be an interest given to them with safety to the kingdom, others do think that no part of their interest could be given without destruction to the kingdom.

Wildman, addressing Ireton: For the matter of stating the thing in difference, I think that the person of king and Lords are not so joined together by any; for as yourself said, none have any exception against the persons of the Lords or name of Lords. But the difference is whether we should after the old foundations of our government so as to give to king and Lords that which they could never claim before. Whereas it's said that those that dissent to giving king and Lords a negative voice look after alteration of government, I do rather think that those that do assent do endeavour to alter the foundations of our government, and that I shall demonstrate thus. According to the king's oath he is to grant such laws as the people shall choose, and therefore I conceive they are called laws before they come to him. They are called laws that he must confirm, and so they are laws before they come to him. To give the king a legislative power is contrary to his own oath at his coronation, and it is the like to give a power to the king by his negative voice to deny all laws. And for the Lords, seeing the foundation of all justice is the election of the people, it is unjust that they should have that power. And therefore I conceive the difference only is this: whether this power should be given to the king and Lords or no.

For the later part of that noble gentleman's words, this may be said to them: whether this consideration may not be paramount to all engagements: to give the people what is their due right. [. . .]

[The day's discussion ended with a motion to return on the morrow, but the record of the remaining days of the debates is only fragmentary. On 8 November the army's commanders, perhaps alarmed at the extent of the support for the 'Agreement', moved to bring the debating to an end by proposing that the agitators should return to their regiments. There apparently was no opposition to this motion, and the final meeting of a council committee at Putney took place three days later.]

have to offer for discovery and prevention of so great a danger. And because we have been the first movers in and concerning an agreement of the people as the most proper and just means for the settling the long and tedious distractions of this nation occasioned by nothing more than the uncertainty of our government, and since there has been an 'Agreement' prepared and presented by some officers of the army to this honourable House,[2] as what they thought requisite to be agreed unto by the people (you approving thereof), we shall in the first place deliver our apprehensions thereupon.

That an agreement between those that trust and those who are trusted has appeared a thing acceptable to this honourable House, his Excellency,[3] and the officers of the army, is much to our rejoicing, as we conceive it just in itself and profitable for the commonwealth, and cannot doubt but that you will protect those of the people who have no ways forfeited their birthright in their proper liberty of taking this or any other agreement as God and their own considerations shall direct them. Which we the rather mention, for that many particulars in the 'Agreement' before you, are upon serious examination thereof dissatisfactory to most of those who are very earnestly desirous of an agreement; and many very material things seem to be wanting therein, which may be supplied in another. As:[4]

1. They are now much troubled there should be any intervals between the ending of this representative and the beginning of the next, as being desirous that this present Parliament – that has lately done so great things in so short a time tending to their liberties – should sit until with certainty and safety they can see them delivered into the hands of another representative, rather than to leave them (though never so small a time) under the dominion of a council of state: a constitution of a new and inexperienced nature, and which they fear as the case now stands may design to perpetuate their power and to keep off Parliaments for ever.

2. They now conceive no less danger in that it is provided that Parliaments for the future are to continue but 6 months, and a council of state 18. In which time, if they should prove corrupt, having command of all forces by sea and land, they will have great opportunities to make themselves absolute and unaccountable. And because this is a danger than which there cannot well be a greater, they generally incline to annual Parliaments, bounded and limited as reason shall devise, not dissolvable, but to be continued or adjourned as shall seem good in their discretion during that year, but no longer, and then to dissolve of course and give

way to those who shall be chosen immediately to succeed them; and in the intervals of their adjournments, to entrust an ordinary committee of their own members, as in other cases limited and bounded with express instructions and accountable to the next session, which will avoid all those dangers feared from a council of state as at present this is constituted.

3. They are not satisfied with the clause wherein it is said that the power of the representatives shall extend 'to the erecting and abolishing of courts of justice', since the alteration of the usual way of trials by twelve sworn men of the neighbourhood may be included therein, a constitution so equal and just in itself as that they conceive it ought to remain unalterable. Neither is it clear what is meant by these words, viz. that the representatives have 'the highest final judgement', they conceiving that their authority in these cases is only to make laws, rules and directions for other courts and persons assigned by law for the execution thereof; unto which every member of the commonwealth, as well those of the representative as others, should be alike subject, it being likewise unreasonable in itself, and an occasion of much partiality, injustice and vexation to the people that the lawmakers should be law-executors.

4. Although it does provide that in the 'laws hereafter to be made, no person by virtue of any tenure, grant, charter, patent, degree or birth, shall be privileged from subjection thereto, or from being bound thereby, as well as others', yet does it not null and make void those present protections by law, or otherwise; nor leave all persons, as well lords as others, alike liable in person and estate, as in reason and conscience they ought to be.

5. They are very much unsatisfied with what is expressed as a reserve from the representative in matters of religion, as being very obscure and full of perplexity, that ought to be most plain and clear, there having occurred no greater trouble to the nation about anything than by the intermeddling of Parliaments in matters of religion.

6. They seem to conceive it absolutely necessary that there be in their agreement a reserve from ever having any kingly government, and a bar against restoring the House of Lords, both which are wanting in the 'Agreement' which is before you.

7. They seem to be resolved to take away all known and burdensome grievances, as tithes (that great oppression of the country's industry and hindrance of tillage), excise and customs (those secret thieves and robbers, drainers of the poor and middle sort of people, and the greatest

obstructers of trade, surmounting all the prejudices of ship money, patents and projects before this Parliament); also to take away all monopolising companies of merchants (the hinderers and decayers of clothing and cloth-working, dyeing, and the like useful professions) by which thousands of poor people might be set at work that are now ready to starve, were merchandising restored to its due and proper freedom. They conceive likewise that the three grievances before mentioned, viz. monopolising companies, excise and customs, do exceedingly prejudice shipping and navigation and consequently discourage sea-men and mariners, and which have had no small influence upon the late unhappy revolts which have so much endangered the nation and so much advantaged your enemies.[5] They also incline to direct a more equal and less burdensome way for levying monies for the future, those other fore-mentioned being so chargeable in the receipt as that the very stipends and allowance to the officers attending thereupon would defray a very great part of the charge of the army, whereas now they engender and support a corrupt interest. They also have in mind to take away all imprisonment of disabled men for debt and to provide some effectual course to enforce all that are able to a speedy payment, and not suffer them to be sheltered in prisons where they live in plenty whilst their creditors are undone. They have also in mind to provide work and comfortable maintenance for all sorts of poor, aged and impotent people, and to establish some more speedy, less troublesome and chargeable way for deciding of controversies in law (whole families having been ruined by seeking right in the ways yet in being). All which, though of greatest and most immediate concernment to the people, are yet omitted in their 'Agreement' before you.

These and the like are their intentions in what they purpose for an agreement of the people, as being resolved (so far as they are able) to lay an impossibility upon all whom they shall hereafter trust of ever wronging the commonwealth in any considerable measure without certainty of ruining themselves, and as conceiving it to be an improper, tedious and unprofitable thing for the people to be ever running after their representatives with petitions for redress of such grievances as may at once be removed by themselves, or to depend for these things so essential to their happiness and freedom upon the uncertain judgements of successive representatives, the one being apt to renew what the other has taken away.

And as to the use of their rights and liberties herein, as becomes and is due to the people from whom all just powers are derived, they hoped for and expect what protection is in you and the army to afford. And we likewise in their and our own behalves do earnestly desire that you will publicly declare your resolution to protect those who have not forfeited their liberties[6] in the use thereof, lest they should conceive that the 'Agreement' before you, being published abroad and the commissioners therein nominated being at work in pursuance thereof, is intended to be imposed upon them, which, as it is absolutely contrary to the nature of a free agreement, so we are persuaded it cannot enter into your thoughts to use any impulsion therein.

But although we have presented our apprehensions and desires concerning this great work of an agreement and are apt to persuade ourselves that nothing shall be able to frustrate our hopes which we have built thereupon, yet have we seen and heard many things of late which occasion not only apprehensions of other matters intended to be brought upon us of danger to such an agreement but of bondage and ruin to all such as shall pursue it. In so much that we are even aghast and astonished to see that notwithstanding the productions of the highest notions of freedom that ever this nation, or any people in the world, have brought to light, notwithstanding the vast expense of blood and treasure that has been made to purchase those freedoms, notwithstanding the many eminent and even miraculous victories God has been pleased to honour our just cause withal, notwithstanding the extraordinary gripes and pangs this House has suffered more than once at the hands of your own servants, and that at least seemingly for the obtaining these our native liberties. When we consider what rackings and tortures the people in general have suffered through decay of trade and dearness of food, and very many families in particular (through free quarter, violence and other miseries incident to war) having nothing to support them therein but hopes of freedom and a well-settled commonwealth in the end: that yet after all these things have been done and suffered, and whilst the way of an agreement of the people is owned and approved, even by yourselves, and that all men are in expectation of being put into possession of so dear a purchase, behold, in the close of all, we hear and see what gives us fresh and pregnant cause to believe that the contrary is really intended and that all those specious pretences and high notions of liberty, with those extraordinary courses that have of late been taken (as if of necessity for liberty, and which indeed can never be justified but deserve the greatest punishments unless they end in just liberty and an equal government) appear to us to have been done and directed by some secret, powerful influences, the more securely and unsuspectedly to attain an absolute domination over the commonwealth; it being impossible for them, but by assuming our generally approved principles and hiding under the fair show thereof their other designs, to have drawn in so many good and godly men (really aiming at what the other had but in show and pretence) and making them unwittingly instrumental to their own and their country's bondage.

For where is that good, or where is that liberty so much pretended, so dearly purchased, if we look upon what this House has done since it has voted itself the supreme authority and disburdened themselves of the power of the Lords?[7]

First, we find a High Court of Justice erected for trial of criminal causes, whereby that great and stronghold of our preservation, the way of trial by twelve sworn men of the neighbourhood, is infringed; all liberty of exception against the triers is overruled by a court consisting of persons picked and chosen in an unusual way, the practice whereof we cannot allow of, though against open and notorious enemies, as well because we know it to be an usual policy to introduce by such means all usurpations, first against adversaries, in hope of easier admission; as also, for that the same being so admitted, may at pleasure be exercised against any person or persons whatsoever. This is the first part of our new liberty.

The next is the censuring of a member of this House for declaring his judgement in a point of religion,[8] which is directly opposite to the reserve in the 'Agreement' concerning religion. Besides the Act for pressing of seamen, directly contrary to the 'Agreement' of the officers. Then the stopping of our mouths from printing is carefully provided for, and the most severe and unreasonable ordinances of Parliament that were made in the time of Holles and Stapleton's reign to gag us from speaking truth and discovering the tyrannies of bad men are referred to the care of the general, and by him to his marshal, to be put in execution in searching, fining, imprisoning and other ways corporally punishing all that any ways be guilty of unlicensed printing; they dealing with us as the bishops of old did with the honest puritan, who were exact in getting laws made against the papist, but really intended them against the puritan, and made them feel the smart of them: which also has been, and is daily exercised most violently, whereby our liberties have been more deeply wounded than since the beginning of this Parliament, and that to the dislike of the soldiery, as by their late petition in that behalf plainly appears.[9] Then whereas it was expected that the Chancery, and courts of justice in Westminster, and the judges and officers thereof, should have been surveyed, and for the present regulated till a better and more equal way of deciding controversies could have been constituted, that the trouble and charge of the people in their suits should have been abated: instead hereof, the old and advanced fees are continued, and new thousand pounds' annual stipends allotted (when in the corruptest times the ordinary fees were thought a great and a sore burden). In the mean time, and in lieu thereof, there is not one perplexity or absurdity in proceedings taken away.

Those petitioners that have moved in behalf of the people, how have they been entertained? Sometimes with the compliment of empty thanks, their desires in the mean time not at all considered; at other times meeting with reproaches and threats for their constancy and public affections, and with violent motions that their petitions be burnt by the common hangman, whilst others are not taken in at all: to so small an account are the people brought, even while they are flattered with notions of being 'the original of all just power'.

And lastly, for completing this new kind of liberty, a council of state is hastily erected for guardians thereof,[10] who to that end are possessed with power to order and dispose all the forces appertaining to England by sea or land, to dispose of the public treasure, to command any person whatsoever before them, to give oath for the discovering of truth, to imprison any that shall disobey their commands, and such as they shall judge contumacious.[11] What now is become of that liberty that no man's person shall be attached or imprisoned, or otherwise dis-seized of his freehold, or free customs, but by lawful judgement of his equals?

We entreat you give us leave to lay these things open to your view and judge impartially of our present condition, and of your own also, that by strong and powerful influences of some persons, are put upon these and the like proceedings, which both you and we before long (if we look not to it) shall be enforced to subject ourselves unto.

Then we have further cause to complain when we consider the persons.[12] As first: the chief of the army, directly contrary to what themselves thought meet in their 'Agreement of the people'. Second, judges of the law and treasures for monies. Then 5 that were members of the Lords' House, and most of them such as have refused to approve of your votes and proceedings, concerning the king and Lords, and 2 of them judges in the Star Chamber, and approvers of the bloody and tyrannical sentences issuing from thence. Some of your own House, forward men in the treaty, and decliners of your last proceedings.[13] All which do clearly manifest to our understandings that the secret contrivers of those things do think themselves now so surely guarded by the strength of an army, by their daily acts and stratagems to their ends inclined, and the captivation of this House, that they may now take off the veil and cloak of their designs as dreadless of whatever can be done against them.

By this council of state, all power is got into their own hands – a project which has been long and industriously laboured for, and which being once firmly and to their liking established, their next motions may be (upon pretence of ease to the people) for the dissolution of this Parliament, half of whose time is already swallowed up by the said council now – because no obstacle lies in their way to the full establishment of these their ends but the uncorrupted part of the soldiery that have their eyes fixed upon their engagements and promises of good to the people and resolve by no threats or allurements to decline the same, together with that part of the people in the city and counties that remain constant in their motions for common good and still persist to run their utmost hazards for procurement of the same, by whom all evil men's designs both have, and are still likely to, find a check and discovery.

Hereupon the grand contrivers fore-mentioned, whom we can particular by name,[14] do begin to raise their spleen and manifest a more violent enmity against soldiers and people, disposed as aforesaid, than ever heretofore, as appears by what lately passed at a meeting of officers on February 22 last at Whitehall, where, after expressions of much bitterness against the most conscientious part of the soldiery and others, it was insisted upon (as we are from very credible hands certainly informed) that a motion should be made to this House for the procurement of a law enabling them to put to death all such as they should judge by petitions or otherwise to disturb the present proceedings. And upon urging that the civil magistrate should do it, it was answered, that they could hang twenty before the magistrate one. It was likewise urged that orders might be given to seize upon the petitioners, soldiers or others at their meetings – with much exclamation against some of greatest integrity to your just authority, whereof they have given continual and undeniable assurances. A proclamation was likewise appointed forbidding the soldiers to petition you, or any but their officers, and prohibiting their correspondences; and private orders to be given out for seizing upon citizens and soldiers at their meetings.

And thus after these fair blossoms of hopeful liberty breaks forth this bitter fruit of the vilest and basest bondage that ever Englishmen groaned under, whereby this, notwithstanding, is gained viz. an evident and (we hope) a timely discovery of the instruments from whence all the evils, contrivances and designs (which for above these eighteen months have been strongly suspected) took their rise and original, even ever since the first breach of their promises and engagements made at Newmarket and Triploe Heath with the agitators and people. It being for these ends that they have so violently opposed all such as manifested any zeal for common right or any regard to the faith of the army, sentencing some to death, others to reproachful punishments, placing and displacing officers according as they showed themselves serviceable or opposite to their designs, enlisting as many as they thought good, even of such as have served in arms against you. And then again, upon pretence of easing the charge of the people, disbanding supernumeraries, by advantage thereof picking out such as were most cordial and active for common good, thereby moulding the army as far as they could to their own bent and ends premised; exercising martial law with much cruelty, thereby to debase their spirits and make them subservient to their wills and pleasures; extending likewise their power (in many cases) over persons not members of the army.

And when, in case of opposition and difficult services, they have by their creatures desired a reconciliation with such as at other times they reproached, vilified and otherwise abased, and through fair promises of good (and dissembled repentance) gained their association and assistance to the great advantage of their proceedings, yet – their necessities being over and the common enemy subdued – they have slighted their former promises and renewed their hate and bitterness against such their assistances, reproaching them with such appellations as they knew did most distaste the people, such as Levellers, Jesuits, anarchists, royalists – names both contradictory in themselves and altogether groundless in relation to the men so reputed; merely relying for belief thereof upon the easiness and credulity of the people. And though, the better to insinuate themselves and get repute with the people, as also to conquer their necessities, they have been fain to make use of those very principles and productions the men they have so much traduced have brought to light, yet the producers themselves they have and do still more eagerly malign than ever, as such whom they know to be acquainted to their deceits and deviations and best able to discover the same.

So that now at length, guessing all to be sure and their own (the king being removed, the House of Lords nulled, their long-plotted council of state erected and this House awed to their ends), the edge of their malice is turning against such as have yet so much courage left them as to appear for the well-establishment of England's liberties. And because God has preserved a great part of the army untainted with the guilt of the designs aforementioned, who cannot without much danger to the designers themselves be suppressed, they have resolved to put this House upon raising more new forces (notwithstanding the present necessities of the people in maintaining those that are already); in doing whereof, though the pretence be danger and opposition, yet the concealed end is like to be the over-balancing those in the army who are resolved to stand for true freedom as the end of all their labours, the which (if they should be permitted to do) they would not then doubt of making themselves absolute seizures,[15] lords and masters, both of Parliament and people; which, when they have done, we expect the utmost of misery. Nor shall it grieve us to expire with the liberties of our native country. For what good man can with any comfort to himself survive then?

But God has hitherto preserved us; and the justice of our desires, as integrity of our intentions, are daily more and more manifest to the impartial and unprejudiced part of men; in so much that it is no small comfort to us that – notwithstanding we are upon all these disadvantages that may be, having neither power nor pre-eminence (the common idols of the world) – our cause and principles do through their own natural truth and lustre get ground in men's understandings; so that where there was one, twelve months since, that owned our principles, we believe there are now hundreds: so that though we fail, our truths prosper.

And posterity we doubt not shall reap the benefit of our endeavours whatever shall become of us. However, though we have neither strength nor safety before us, we have discharged our consciences and emptied our breasts unto you, knowing well that if you will make use of your power and take unto you that courage which becomes men of your trust and condition, you may yet through the goodness of God prevent the danger and mischief intended and be instrumental in restoring this long-enthralled and betrayed nation into a good and happy condition. For which end we most earnestly desire and propose, as the main prop and support of the work:

1. That you will not dissolve this House nor suffer yourselves to be dissolved until as aforesaid you see a new representative the next day

ready to take your room; which you may confidently and safely insist upon, there being no considerable number in the army or elsewhere that will be so unworthy as to dare to disturb you therein.

2. That you will put in practice the Self-denying Ordinance,[16] the most just and useful that ever was made, and continually cried out for by the people, whereby a great infamy that lies upon your cause will be removed, and men of powerful influences and dangerous designs, deprived of those means and opportunities which now they have to prejudice the public.

3. That you will consider how dangerous it is for one and the same persons to be continued long in the highest commands of a military power, especially acting so long distinct and of themselves as those now in being have done, and in such extraordinary ways whereunto they have accustomed themselves, which was the original of most regalities and tyrannies in the world.

4. That you appoint a committee of such of your own members as have been longest established upon those rules of freedom upon which you now proceed to hear, examine and conclude all controversies between officers and officers, and between officers and soldiers; to consider and mitigate the law-martial, and to provide that it be not exercised at all upon persons not of the army; also to release and repair such as have thereby unduly suffered, as they shall see cause; to consider the condition of the private soldiers, both horse and foot, in these dear times, and to allow them such increase of pay as wherewithal they may live comfortably, and honestly discharge their quarters. That all disbanding be referred to the said committee, and that such of the army as have served the king may be first disbanded.

5. That you will open the press, whereby all treacherous and tyrannical designs may be the easier discovered and so prevented, which is a liberty of greatest concernment to the commonwealth, and which such only as intend a tyranny are engaged to prohibit: the mouths of adversaries being best stopped by the sensible good which the people receive from the actions of such as are in authority.

6. That you will (whilst you have opportunity) abate the charge of the law, and reduce the stipends of judges and all other magistrates and officers in the commonwealth to a less, but competent, allowance, converting the over-plus to the public treasury, whereby the taxes of the people may be much eased.

7. But above all that you will dissolve this present council of state,

which upon the grounds fore-mentioned so much threatens tyranny, and manage your affairs by committees of short continuance and such as may be frequently and exactly accountable for the discharge of their trusts.

8. That you will publish a strict prohibition and severe penalty against all such, whether committees, magistrates or officers of what kind so ever, as shall exceed the limits of their commission, rules or directions; and encourage all men in their informations and complaints against them.

9. That you will speedily satisfy the expectations of the soldiers in point of arrears, and of the people in point of accounts, in such a manner as that it may not (as formerly) prove a snare to such as have been most faithful, and a protection to the most corrupt in the discharge of their trust and duties.

10. That the so-many-times complained of Ordinance for Tithes upon treble damages may be forthwith taken away.

All which, together with due regard showed to petitioners, without respect to their number and strength, would so fasten you in the affections of the people and of the honest officers and soldiers, as that you should not need to fear any opposite power whatsoever, and for the time to come of yourselves enjoy the exercise of your supreme authority whereof you have yet but the name only, and be enabled to vindicate your just undertakings; wherein we should not only rejoice to have occasion to manifest how ready we should be to hazard our lives in your behalf, but should also bend all our studies and endeavours to render you honourable to all future generations.

February 26 1648: Being ushered in by the Sergeant-at-Arms, and called to the bar, with all due respects given unto the House, Lieutenant-Colonel John Lilburne, with divers others coming to the bar next the mace, with the address in his hand, spoke these words, or to this effect, as follows:

Mr Speaker,

I am very glad that without any inconvenience unto myself and those that are with me, I may freely and cheerfully address myself to this honourable House as the supreme authority of England. Time was when I could not, and it much refreshes my spirit to live to see this day that you have made such a step to the people's liberties as to own and declare yourselves to be (as indeed you are) the supreme authority of this nation.

Mr Speaker, I am desired by a company of honest men living in and about London, who in truth do rightly appropriate to themselves the title of the contrivers, promoters, presenters and approvers of the late large London petition of 11 September last (which was the first petition I know of in England that was presented to this honourable House against the late destructive personal treaty with the late king) to present you with their serious apprehensions. And give me leave (I beseech you) for myself and them to say thus much: that for the most part of us, we are those that in the worst of times do own our liberties and freedoms in the face of the greatest of our adversaries, and from the beginning of these wars never shrunk from the owning of our freedoms in the most tempestuous times, nor changed our principles. Sir, let me with truth tell you that to the most of us, our wives, our children, our estates, our relations, our lives and all that upon earth we can call ours, have not been so highly valued by us as our liberties and freedoms; which our constant actions (to the apparent hazard of our blood and lives) have been a clear and full demonstration of for these many years together.

And Mr Speaker, give me leave to tell you that I am confident our liberties and freedoms (the true and just end of all the late wars) are so dear and precious to us that we had rather our lives should breath out with them than to live one moment after the expiration of them.

Mr Speaker, I must confess I am to present you with a paper, something of a new kind, for we have had no longer time to consider of it than from Thursday last; and warrants (as we are informed) issuing out against us to take us, from those that have no power over us, we do not well go our ordinary way to work to get subscriptions to it, lest we should be surprised before we could present it to this honourable House, and so be frustrated in that benefit or relief that we justly expect from you. And to present it with a few hands, we judged inconsiderable in your estimation, and therefore choose in the third place (being in so much haste as we were to prevent our eminent and too apparent ruin) in person to bring it to your bar, and avowedly to present it here. And therefore without any further question, give me leave to tell you I own it, and I know so do all the rest of my friends present; and if any hazard should ensue thereby, give me leave resolvedly to tell you I am sorry I have but one life to lose in maintaining the truth, justice and right-eousness of so gallant a piece.

Mr Speaker, we own this honourable House (as of right), the true guardian of our liberties and freedoms; and we wish and most heartily desire you would rouse up your spirits (like men of gallantry) and now at last take unto yourselves a magnanimous resolution to acquit yourselves (without fear or dread) like the chosen and betrusted trustees of the people, from whom (as yourselves acknowledge and declare) all just power is derived, to free us from all bondage and slavery and really and truly invest us into the price of all our blood, hazards and toils: our liberties and freedoms, the true difference and distinction of men from beasts.

Mr Speaker, though my spirit is full in the sad apprehension of the dying condition of our liberties and freedoms, yet at present I shall say no more, but in the behalf of myself and my friends I shall earnestly entreat you to read these our serious apprehensions seriously and debate them deliberately.

Friends,

This we have adventured to publish for the timely information and benefit of all that adhere unto the common interest of the people, hoping that with such, upon due consideration, it will find as large an acceptance as our late petition of September 11 1648. And we thought good (in regard we were not called in to receive an answer to the same) to acquaint you that we intend to second it with a petition sufficiently subscribed, we doubt not with many thousands, earnestly to solicit for an effectual answer.

NOTES

INTRODUCTION

1 *The Governance of Britain*, July 2007, Cm 7170.
2 'An Agreement of the People', Text 6 below, Preamble.
3 Department of Education and Skills, http://www.standards.dfes.gov.uk.
4 The most commonly quoted version of the encounter is in Lord Campbell, *Lives of the Chief Justice*, 2nd edn, Oxford: Oxford University Press, 1858, p. 272 nd.
5 See Edward Hyde, Earl of Clarendon, *The History of the Rebellion and Civil Wars in England*, Vol. 1, Oxford: Oxford University Press, 1888 (reprinted 2001), p. 5. Clarendon regarded the king's 'unseasonable, unskilful and precipitate' dissolution of parliament as the basic cause of the civil war.
6 See Pauline Gregg, *Freeborn John – The Biography of John Lilburne* (Phoenix Press, 2000), p52–75
7 See Blair Worden, *The Levellers: the Emergence of the term* in Mendle (ed.) *The Putney Debates of 1647* (Cambridge University Press, 2001), p280–2
8 A.S.P. Woodhouse, *Introduction to Puritanism and Liberty, the Army Debates 1647–9* [1938], London: J.M. Dent/Everyman, 1992, p. 24.
9 See Gregg, p. 190.
10 See Austin Woolrych, *Britain in Revolution 1625–1660*, Oxford: Oxford University Press, 2002, p. 385.
11 The Agitators reported to their regiments that 'there were but three voices against this your native freedom'. See Woodhouse, p. 452.
12 Lilburne, *Jonah's Cry*, p. 4.
13 See Geoffrey Robertson QC, *The Tyrannicide Brief: The Story of the Man Who Sent Charles I to the Scaffold*, London: Chatto and Windus, 2005, Chapters 9–11.
14 *Ibid.*, pp. 217–23.
15 *Ibid.*, pp. 247–8.
16 See Geoffrey Robertson QC, *Crimes against Humanity: The Struggle for Global Justice*, 3rd edn, London: Penguin, 2006, pp. 192–6.

I A REMONSTRANCE OF MANY THOUSAND CITIZENS

1   See Glossary.
2   See Glossary.
3   See 'Long Parliament' in Glossary.
4   *ad bene placitum* = by their good pleasure.
5   This was not in fact the case, although there were statutory precedents in support of such a claim. However, since the Triennial Act of 1641, a Parliament was to be called once at least every three years.
6   Wonderful = strange.
7   In 1603 James VI of Scotland became also James I of England, despite having a claim to the English throne that was open to dispute.
8   Parliament's 'Grand Remonstrance' of 1641, a lengthy list of the inequities of Charles I's reign.
9   This refers to the king's alleged designs of the early 1640s to use either the army he had raised for the war against Scotland or Irish troops to suppress his Parliamentary opponents.
10   In 1642 Charles failed to arrest five members of the Commons on charges of treason.
11   Sottish = foolish.
12   All Parliament-men were immune from civil actions during Parliamentary sessions, but the peerage and their families and servants were generally thought never to be liable.
13   See Glossary.
14   Larner (*d.* 1672), was a printer, publisher and bookseller who produced a number of Leveller works and actively took part in their campaign. As a result he suffered periods of imprisonment.
15   Prerogative courts abolished by Parliament in 1641.
16   A tax collected without Parliamentary consent, which was declared illegal in 1641.
17   Travail = painful effort.
18   A reference to the forces of evil, often identified with the Anti-Christ and popery.
19   The Earl of Strafford (1593-1641), one of the king's closest advisors, was executed by Parliament.
20   A list of Parliamentarian military defeats in the civil war. County Associations combined the forces of separate county armies.
21   Defendants refused to answer questions put to them directly under oath on the grounds that they were being forced to condemn themselves and thereby violate God's command that no man should endanger himself.
22   Sir Henry Garway, Lord Mayor of London, 1639–1640.
23   A complaint against trading and industrial monopolies.

24 This refers to the capture of merchants by pirates in countries such as Algiers.
25 Deem = judge.
26 The excise was a tax upon luxury but also many staple goods (e.g. alcohol, meat and salt), while weekly or monthly assessments were, in effect, land taxes.
27 See Glossary.
28 The 'Solemn League and Covenant', the alliance formed between Parliament and the Scottish Covenanters in 1643, called for the preservation and defence of the king in its third clause.
29 The Anakims were giants who, despite their fearful size, were defeated by the Israelites.

2 THE LARGE PETITION

1 See Glossary.
2 For example, after Charles I ruled for eleven years without Parliament, the assembly met in April 1640 only to be dissolved by the king in the following month.
3 On the meeting of the Long Parliament in November 1640, many puritan exiles thought it safe to return to England.
4 Lilburne was among those imprisoned by the bishops who gained their release.
5 For example, see chapter 1, note 19, above.
6 Bishops were excluded from the Lords in 1642; episcopacy – government of the Church of England by bishops – was abolished in 1646.
7 The tax of one tenth of an individual's annual produce of labour or land taken in support of the established church and its ministry. The desired alternative was a system of voluntary contributions.
8 This refers to attempts to make all public office-holders take the Solemn League and Covenant, which pointed to a restrictive Presbyterian church settlement, thereby essentially disabling nonconformists on grounds of conscience.
9 A complaint that neutrals, former Royalists and those eager for a settlement with the king remained in public office.
10 This refers to the desire of the Presbyterian faction within Parliament to disband the New Model Army.

3 EXTRACTS FROM 'THE HEADS OF THE PROPOSALS'

1 See Glossary.
2 See 'General Council of the Army' in Glossary.

3 See 'Army Engagements' in Glossary.
4 Clause III of the 'Proposals' provided for the creation of a council of state in place of a traditional privy council.
5 The concern here was to ensure that all soldiers would remain free from criminal prosecution for acts committed during the war.
6 *ex officio* = by virtue of office.
7 Under clause XV only five persons were totally excepted from pardon.
8 Punitive fines levied on supporters of the king.
9 There follows a list of separately numbered issues which largely correspond to points 3-4 and 6-10 in chapter 2, above.

4 EXTRACTS FROM 'THE CASE OF THE ARMY TRULY STATED'

1 See Glossary.
2 The petition addressed the army's material concerns and was circulating for subscription by March 1647.
3 I.e. the General Council of the Army.
4 See Glossary.
5 There follows a series of numbered demands which cover much the same ground as points 3-4, 6-10 and 12 in chapter 2, above.
6 See Glossary for Everard. Relatively little is known of the other agents.

5 EXTRACTS FROM 'A CALL TO ALL THE SOLDIERS OF THE ARMY'

1 See Glossary.
2 Vizards = masks.
3 See Glossary.
4 See Glossary.
5 *ad terrorem* = to the fear. However, the accusation made was a false one.
6 Abroad = elsewhere, in different locations.
7 Meetest = most suitable.
8 Denzil Holles (1598-1680) and Sir Philip Stapleton (1603-1647), the architects of the Presbyterian design to disband the New Model.
9 The practice whereby householders provided soldiers with board and lodging, in exchange for a ticket that might later be redeemed for money.
10 John Ashburnham (1602/3-1671), one of the king's courtiers.
11 Prior to the army's 'Solemn engagement', the soldiers had established an organisation for their defence at Bury St Edmunds.

6 AN AGREEMENT OF THE PEOPLE

1 A false claim that appeared on the printed version of the 'Agreement', which reached London bookstalls by early November.
2 I.e. Charles I.
3 See chapter 1, note 5, above; and chapter 2, note 2, above.

7 EXTRACTS FROM 'THE PUTNEY DEBATES'

1 See Glossary.
2 Robert Everard.
3 I.e. Everard; see Glossary.
4 I.e. himself and another, unnamed agent.
5 John Wildman and Maximilian Petty; see Glossary.
6 See Glossary.
7 Cowling was an agitator and commissary-general of victuals in the artillery train.
8 At the time there was no universal qualification for the Parliamentary franchise. In county constituencies there existed a uniform 40 shilling freehold franchise, but in cities and boroughs the qualifications varied widely. Some merely enfranchised a wealthy elite, while others might incorporate wage-earners and labourers.
9 I.e. through his involvement in drafting 'The Heads of the Proposals'; see chapter 3, clause I, no. 5, above.
10 Rich (*d.*1701?) was the colonel of a New Model horse regiment.
11 A reference to the convention of primogeniture, by which eldest sons of gentry families inherited their fathers' estates, while younger sons were forced to seek professional occupations.
12 Rainborough (*fl.*1639–1673), younger brother of Thomas, was an agitator in Colonel Thomas Harrison's horse regiment.
13 I.e. Colonel Rich.
14 A point made earlier during the prayer meeting.
15 Peter (1598–1660), was chaplain to the artillery train.
16 I.e. the poor insignificant people – 'scrubs' – will be impressed to fight on the behalf of the rich.
17 Denizen = citizen.
18 Clarke (*fl.*1645–1660) was an agitator in Sir Hardress Waller's foot regiment.
19 Read (*d.*1662) of Cromwell's horse regiment.
20 *Sic volo, sic jubeo* = thus I will, thus I command.
21 Allen (*fl.*1642–1667), was an agitator and trooper in Cromwell's horse regiment.

22 I.e. William Allen.
23 Bishop (*d.* 1668) became a Quaker in the 1650s.
24 I.e. the king.
25 I.e. Cromwell.

8 ENGLAND'S NEW CHAINS DISCOVERED

1   A petition that comprehensively set out the Leveller programme. It received support from sections of the army and was claimed by the Levellers to have attracted 40,000 signatories.
2   The so-called 'Officers agreement', which was presented to the Commons in January 1649 but was thereafter never discussed. The Levellers participated in the drafting of this 'Agreement', but turned their backs on it when the army's commanders subjected it to further discussion and amendment.
3   I.e. Fairfax.
4   The following numbered points are explicit criticisms of the content of the 'Officers agreement'.
5   A reference to the second civil war.
6   I.e. Royalists and those who had sought an accommodation with the king.
7   In January 1649 the Commons voted itself the supreme authority in the nation and claimed that its Acts had the force of law without the concurrence of king or Lords.
8   A reference to the anti-Trinitarian Parliament-man John Fry (1609–1657), who in 1649 was briefly suspended from the Commons.
9   In a petition to the Commons of February 1649, a number of soldiers expressed their opposition to policing the recently approved ordinance against unlicensed printing, which was originally enforced in September 1647.
10 A council of state of forty-one members was nominated and first met in February 1649.
11 Contumacious = insubordinate or disobedient.
12 The following is a complaint against some of the people nominated to sit on the council of state.
13 I.e. those members of the Commons who had either favoured an accommodation with the king or had opposed the regicide and the abolition of the kingship and the Lords.
14 The principle 'grand contrivers' were, of course, Cromwell and Ireton.
15 Seizures = those who lay hold of forcibly.
16 The Self-denying Ordinance of April 1645 was intended to prevent Parliament-men from holding military or civil office during the civil war, though individuals such as Cromwell had long been excepted from its provisions.